Sydney Opera house

Woodslane Press Pty Ltd
7/5 Vuko Place, Warriewood, NSW 2102
Email: info@woodslane.com.au
Website: www.woodslane.com.au

© 2011 Woodslane Press, text and photography © 2011 Derek and Julia Parker

This work is copyright. All rights reserved. Apart from any fair dealing for the purposes of study, research or review, as permitted under Australian copyright law, no part of this publication may be reproduced, distributed, or transmitted in any other form or by any means, including photocopying, recording, or other electronic or mechanical methods, without the prior written permission of the publisher. For permission requests, write to the publisher, addressed "Attention: Permissions Coordinator", at the address above. Every effort has been made to obtain permissions relating to information reproduced in this publication. The information in this publication is based upon the current state of commercial and industry practice and the general circumstances as at the date of publication. No person shall rely on any of the contents of this publication and the publisher and the author expressly exclude all liability for direct and indirect loss suffered by any person resulting in any way from the use or reliance on this publication or any part of it. Any opinions and advice are offered solely in pursuance of the author's and publisher's intention to provide information, and have not been specifically sought.

National Library of Australia Cataloguing-in-Publication entry

Author:	Parker, Derek, 1932-
Title:	Building Sydney's history : structures, sculptures, stories and secrets / Derek Parker, Julia Parker.
ISBN:	9781921683213 (pbk.)
Notes:	Includes index.
Subjects:	Architecture–New South Wales–Sydney–History: Sculpture–New South Wales– Sydney–History: Sydney (N.S.W.)–Buildings, structures, etc.–History.
Other Authors/Contributors:	Parker, Julia, 1932-
Dewey Number:	720.99441

Design and layout by Simon Dance
Printed in China

BUILDING SYDNEY'S HISTORY

STRUCTURES, SCULPTURES, STORIES AND SECRETS

Derek and Julia Parker

CONTENTS

Locations	vi-vii
Introduction	ix
Tank Stream	1
Elizabeth Farm	5
Government House, Parramatta	11
Rocks	19
Cadman's Cottage	25
Rum Hospital	29
Macquarie Place	35
Macquarie's Lighthouse	41
Hyde Park Barracks	43
St James's Church	47
Don Bank	51
Vaucluse House	53
Juniper Hall	57
Quarantine Station	59
Two Schools	65
Experiment Farm Cottage	73
Potts Point	75
Darlinghurst Gaol	79
Admiralty House	85
Government House, Sydney	89
Garrison Church	95
Sydney Observatory	101
Water Police Court	106
Boy Charlton Pool	109
Mortuary Temple	111
Sydney Town Hall	115
Necropolis	123
Fortifications	127
Carisbrook House	131
Eveleigh Railway Yards	133
Callan Park	137
Fort Denison	141
Strand Arcade	145
Queen Victoria Building	149
Boronia House	155
Central Station	157
Finger Wharf	161
Babworth House	165
Commonwealth Bank	169
Ferry Wharves	175
Nutcote	179
Dymock's Building	181
Capitol and State Theatres	187
Bathers Pavilion	189
Harbour Bridge	193
State Library	199
Warragamba Dam	205
Chifley Square	207
Opera House	211
Blues Point Tower	217
Warringah Mall	219
Mapping Sydney's History	223
Sources	229
Index	231
Photography in this book	234
Acknowledgements	234

Building Sydney's History

LOCATIONS

1. Elizabeth Farm
2. Old Government House, Parramatta
3. Cadman's Cottage
4. The Rum Hospital
5. Macquarie Place
6. Macquarie's Lighthouse
7. Hyde Park Barracks
8. St James's Church
9. Don Bank
10. Vaucluse House
11. Juniper Hall
12. The Quarantine Station
13. Two Schools
14. Experiment Farm Cottage
15. Darlinghurst Gaol
16. Admiralty House
17. Government House, Sydney
18. The Garrison Church
19. Sydney Observatory
20. The Water Police Court
21. Boy Charlton Pool
22. Mortuary Temple
23. Sydney Town Hall
24. The Necropolis
25. Carisbrook House
26. Eveleigh Railway Yards
27. Callan Park
28. Fort Denison
29. The Strand Arcade
30. The Queen Victoria Building
31. Boronia House
32. Central Station
33. The Finger Wharf
34. Babworth House
35. Commonwealth Bank
36. Nutcote
37. Dymocks Building
38. Capitol and State Theatres
39. Bathers' Pavilion
40. Sydney Harbour Bridge
41. The State Library
42. Chifley Square
43. The Opera House
44. Blues Point Tower
45. Warringah Mall

See over for map

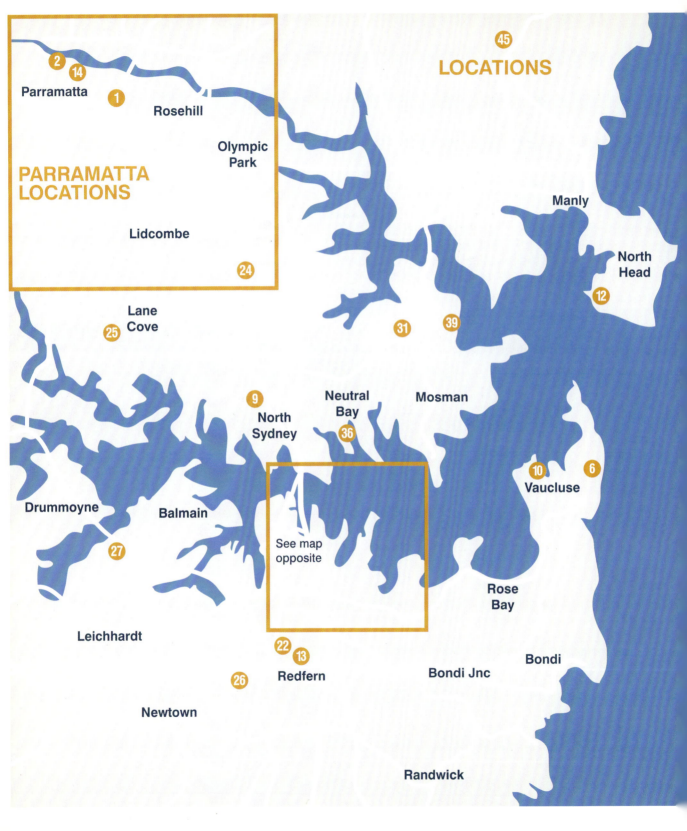

INTRODUCTION

The character of a people is revealed in how they choose to live – the style of government they select, the amusements they prefer, the form of art they encourage, and the buildings in which they spend their time. From the slightly surprising elegance of a convict architect's barracks to a world heritage masterpiece, from a small stone cottage to a boastful art deco mansion, the buildings of Sydney speak of the ambitions and achievements of her citizens over two tumultuous centuries.

Sydney owes much to Governor Lachlan Macquarie, whose vision of the city can still be seen in the general layout of her streets and the ambition of her earliest public buildings. But like every city, she has grown according to the tastes and aspirations of succeeding generations of Sydneysiders – at one moment building a handsome gaol completely unfit for purpose, at another celebrating the fun of cinema-going in a riot of delicious fakery; here creating a great industrial quarter, there turning a market building into the finest shopping mall in the world.

Meanwhile, people were devising their homes, collaborating with professional architects and planners to build cottages and mansions and apartment blocks, and so in building Sydney's history – a history of the city reflecting that of Australia itself. We have tried to chose a selection of buildings which illustrate various aspects of that history from the earliest months of the settlement to a time when the city looks forward with some apprehension to the finalisation of plans for the next great architectural opportunity – the development of the huge space of Barangaroo.

We are grateful to everyone who has given permission for photography; and to those who have allowed us to reproduce photographs from what seems an increasingly remote past.

THE TANK STREAM

But for the Tank Stream, Sydney would be somewhere else.

Having sailed the First Fleet to Botany Bay, recommended to him as 'an ideal pace for a convict settlement', Capt. Arthur Phillip discovered that it consisted of a swamp served by waters too shallow for ships to berth inshore.

Happily, just around the corner to the north, he discovered the waters of Port Jackson – 'the finest harbour in the world' – and within them a bay where there was (as his companion Capt. David Collins later wrote) a 'run of fresh water, which stole silently along through a very thick wood, the stillness of which had then, for the first time since the creation, been interrupted by the rude sound of the labourer's axe, and the downfall of its ancient inhabitants.'[1]

The stream rose in swampy ground not far inland and ran into the harbour some distance south of what is now Circular Quay. Around it Phillip pitched his tents, with Government House (his own tent), his staff and guards to the east of the stream and the convicts, marines and hospital to the west.

The stream served the settlement well during its first months; then after two years came the first of a number of severe droughts, and the Governor ordered the construction of three water storage tanks in the neighbourhood of what is now Australia Square. It was at this time that the Tank Stream got its lasting name. As was often the case, ordinary people were no respecters of open streams, and though for a time it was the only source of clean water in Sydney the Tank Stream quickly became an open sewer and a dump for waste, with pigs rooting about in it. It was abandoned with good reason in 1826 in favour of Busby's Bore, the young city's second source of water, built by convicts to carry a supply from swamps near what is now Centennial Park. The water in the Tank Stream diminished as the swamps supplying it were drained; more and more disdained and ignored it was scorned, covered over for most of its length, and more or less vanished from sight.

Today it still runs persistently on under the buildings and pavements of the CBD, trickling gently along the bottom of what is now a storm drain. It may have been generally forgotten, but architects often have to deal with its presence as it announces itself in terms of soggy foundations and rising damp. This was the case during the construction through the 1870s-80s of the neo-classical Sydney GPO building, from high on whose façade Queen Victoria still keeps a brooding eye on Martin Place. The Stream was somewhat insecurely enclosed under the flagstones of the basements; but when the building became a luxury hotel in the 1990s it was more firmly confined to a stainless steel pipe (which runs through the ceiling of the hotel's underground ballroom). Prompted by a somewhat uncharacteristic deference to icons of Sydney's history, the developers preserved a short section of the original conduit, which can be seen on the lower ground floor.

The Historic Houses Trust with Sydney Water organise biannual tours of the remaining underground sections of the Tank Stream, and it is celebrated in two more ways: in the city pavements, at five different sites, glass lights mark its underground course; and emerging at Circular Quay its waters feed John Fairfax's 1981 Tank Stream Fountain with bronze indigenous animals and birds – a delightful fantasy dedicated to 'all children who have played around the Tank Stream'.

[1] David Collins, Account of the English Colony of New South Wales, 1802

The Tank Stream

ELIZABETH FARM

Elizabeth Farm was built by the prominent, and to many controversial ex-army officer John Macarthur for himself and his wife Elizabeth. Macarthur, as paymaster and inspector of public works, knew just who to employ on the building, which in 1793 was both handsome and well-planned, though it comprised only two rooms separated by a hallway. A verandah was swiftly added, then an extra bedroom; other rooms were not an integral part of the house – kitchen and scullery, storerooms and servants' accommodation.

During the last decade of his life Macarthur, mentally unbalanced, became besotted with architecture, and at various times engaged half-a-dozen architects to interpret his own ideas for enlarging the house. In 1826 a bedroom wing was planned and considerable work was done, including lowering the floor to give the rooms extra height. But by then Macarthur, in his wife's words, 'cannot do anything in a quiet, orderly way', and in 1832 he was declared insane and died at Elizabeth Farm two years later, having much altered the house, but with many of his plans unfulfilled.

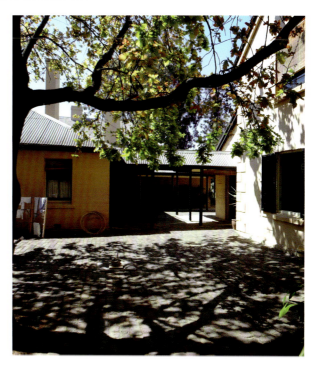

John Macarthur played a notable part in the early history of the colony. An army lieutenant, he became one of the foremost landowners and wool producers in the colony. Quarrels with authority enhanced rather than hindered the growth of his wealth, which enabled him not only to build Elizabeth Farm on four hundred acres granted him au Parromaúa by the Governor, but a large house at Camden Park, where he eventually held sixty thousand acres. He also built in 1824 a second house at Parramatta, Hambledon Cottage, also now open to the public. Towards the end of his life his architectural fantasies got out of hand both at Elizabeth Farm and Camden Park House (completed a year after his death), but in the former he created a really pleasant, calm and civilised house. Elizabeth Farm has some delightful features such as, for instance, the two little rooms or 'closets' he had constructed, no more than 2.7 metres square, at the east and west ends of the façade, off the dining and drawing rooms – ideal rooms for reading or writing, or simply sitting. As part of the 1826 work, Macarthur enlarged his bedroom, behind the drawing room, making it into 'a handsome library', but due to his increasing insanity further work was never carried out. The room became his 'library-bedroom' in which, sadly, he was eventually forcibly confined until he was transferred to Camden Park House, where he died in the unfinished house in 1834.

The fact that so much of the original structure remains intact (in the Oak Tree room part of the original shingled roof of the house can still be seen) is due to the care expended on the building by the Swann family, who bought it in 1904. William and Elizabeth Swann (and later his daughters) maintained it with such diligence that when the Elizabeth Farm Museum Trust bought it in 1968 it was, though structurally weak, largely unaltered. The Historic Houses Trust now runs it as the best sort of house museum: furnished as nearly as possible as Macarthur and his wife would have furnished it; open to visitors to amble about it in their own time, unhurried and unencumbered by guides; and free to sit in the drawing room or on the balcony and take in the atmosphere of the past, an atmosphere which is noticeably calm and agreeable.

Though little remains of the original garden, a cypress tree sketched by Elizabeth Macarthur still stands, as does an olive tree planted by her husband in 1805.

❶ 70 Alice Street, Rosehill

Home of John Macarthur, th

First N.S.W. "Wool King" 1797

OLD GOVERNMENT HOUSE, PARRAMATTA

The first Government House at Parramatta was a bungalow of lath and plaster 4.2 metres long and 4.8 wide, with outhouses and a storehouse nearby. It was built by Governor Arthur Phillip, but replaced by Governor John Hunter, who built the present house on almost the same site. Governors King and Bligh used this to a greater or lesser degree, but by the time Governor Lachlan Macquarie visited Parramatta with his wife Elizabeth early in 1810 it was in a poor state and needed considerable renovation.

Governor Macquarie talked to his aide-de-camp and friend Lieutenant John Watts about the problem. Watts' experience as an architect was restricted to eighteen months' work with an architectural firm in Dublin, but Macquarie had confidence in him and he ended up designing a barracks, a military hospital and other buildings. During 1815 and 1816 he also worked on the repair and enlargement of Government House at Parramatta, aided by Mrs Macquarie and the convict architect Francis Greenway, whose main contribution was the pretty portico at the entrance.

It would have been be surprising if Elizabeth Macquarie had had no influence on the alterations made to Government House between 1812 and 1818 as she took a serious interest in architecture, and is known to have played a part in designing St John's Church, Parramatta, among other buildings.

Governor Hunter's house had been only one room deep, with an exterior staircase. The building was now enlarged to three times its original size, with a new block seamlessly added at the back of the original building and short colonnades linking two new 'pavilions'. One pavilion contained servants' quarters and the other private rooms for the Governor and his lady: a room for relaxation (combined breakfast, sitting and drawing room) and a handsome bedroom and dressing room.

After the building of the (new) Government House in Sydney in 1845, Governors spent less time at Parramatta, and the house, the oldest public building in Australia, fell into a state of disrepair during the second half of the nineteenth century. During this time is was leased as a school, privately, and also as a boarding house. Probably only its restoration for use as a school (between 1909 and 1967) saved it for the nation, though it was considerably altered by the addition of rooms and outbuildings.

Old Government House, Parramatta

The Government, which still owns the house, eventually entrusted it to the National Trust, and a first stage of restoration was completed in time for Queen Elizabeth II to open it in 1970. Subsequent work has been a model of continued tactful attention, the house returned as nearly as possible to its state when Governor Macquarie and his wife lived in it. Colonial furniture of the correct period has been collected and installed, and the ground floor must appear as nearly in its original state as can be contrived. Volunteer embroiderers and other workers have done remarkable work in restoring furniture and providing curtains and hangings. The drawing room in particular – used by resident Governors for formal entertaining – is especially elegantly furnished. Rooms upstairs house the beginnings of a collection illustrating the social history of the colony.

Elizabeth Macquarie laid out an English garden near the house, with strawberry beds and imported fruit trees, and entertained friends and visitors in a 'beautifully contrived bark hut erected on the hill in the domain', with a pigeon house nearby. Later, Governor Brisbane set up an observatory, and a bath house which was later turned into a pavilion and stands on the hill above the house.

2 Parramatta Park, Parramatta.

Old Government House, Parramatta

THE ROCKS

Why and how certain areas of particular cities establish themselves as disreputable is often obscure, and so it is with the Rocks. Now a centre of the Sydney tourist industry (with highly popular street markets, small boutiques, restaurants and bars), for most of Sydney's history the Rocks was a centre of crime and prostitution.

At first tents, then lath and plaster cottages, and eventually small sandstone houses crowded together in the area bounded by George Street to the east and the Observatory to the west, from Essex Street to the south to Dawes Point to the north. By the time Governor Macquarie arrived in 1809, the Rocks was already the centre of the drinking and whoring trades, and in his very first message to the colony he was forced to speak of 'all species of vice and immorality' taking place in 'the most licentious and disorderly houses'. Within a matter of weeks he had reduced the number of licensed drinking houses from seventy-five to twenty. There are still thirteen heritage pubs in the area, providing a wonderful mixture of architectural styles and atmospheres.

Writing in the 1850s, a London journalist, Frank Fowler, left the most vivid sketch of the Rocks: 'a network of alleys, with houses [many of which] contained only one room with an earth floor, no windows or chimneys, often not even a door. Serpent-like gutters, choked with filth, trail before the tottering tenements, and a decayed water-butt, filled with greasy-looking rain-catchings, stands and rots at the end of each court.' A gang known as the Rocks Push ruled the area with violent possessiveness.

By 1900 it was clear that something had to be done about the area. As well as the problems of crime and violence, most of the houses were derelict and falling down and open drains and communal cesspits threatened disease. Finally, an outbreak of bubonic plague forced the authorities to contemplate the wholesale levelling of the area. Nothing was done during the First

World War but then the building of the Harbour Bridge prompted the demolition of a huge swathe of houses which stood in the way of the southern approach road. The Second World War provided another excuse to do nothing about the area. But in the 1960s the state government once again proposed wholesale demolition and rebuilding, replacing most of the original buildings with high-density housing. Local residents formed a group to oppose the plans, believing that they would completely alter the nature of the area.

The Builders Labourers Federation had in the late sixties become very active in preventing unwanted redevelopment in Sydney, and in 1973 imposed a 'Green Ban' which put a stop to the Sydney Cove Redevelopment Authority's original plans for the area, replacing them with a 'People's Plan'. Although the Liberal government attempted to force through the original scheme by using non-union labour, political defeat replaced them with a more sympathetic Labour government, which recognised public pressure. The result was the present use of the area for tourism and trade with some housing – a few little terraces, together with one or two isolated houses. Warehouses have been converted into restaurants and bars, while the heritage pubs are sufficiently crowded to ensure that the tradition of heavy drinking originally associated mainly with wharfies and seamen is maintained, especially at weekends, by Sydneysiders and tourists. Once famous for prostitution, The Rocks is now largely free of the trade, legal brothels having moved elsewhere.

Globe and Harrington Streets, The Rocks

CADMAN'S COTTAGE

When he was twenty-five years old, John Cadman, who kept an inn in Worcestershire, in England, was found guilty of stealing a horse and sentenced to be transported to Australia 'for the term of his natural life'. He arrived in Sydney in May 1798, and soon made himself useful – by 1809 he was coxswain of a government boat, and seven years later was living in a small sandstone house literally within a stone's throw of the harbour. He stayed there, later with a wife and two children, for eighteen years.

Known now as Cadman's Cottage, this little building is the oldest surviving house in Sydney, and the third oldest building of any kind. It is simple and basic – almost like a child's drawing – and if it is true (as rumour has sometimes asserted) that it was designed by the convict architect Francis Greenway, it is not the most handsome of his achievements. But though its interior is bare and basic, it is a grandparent of every building that followed.

Cadman was fortunate in that Governor Lachlan Macquarie was a firm believer in rewarding good behaviour, and John's diligence was such that in 1814 he was granted a conditional pardon, and moved into the cottage as assistant government coxswain. Though he had probably never seen the sea until he was marched onto a convict transport boat, he somehow contrived to become master of the cutter Mars in 1825, and sailed her to Newcastle with a cargo of twenty-five prisoners.

Later he was given a free pardon, and became superintendent of government boats for Port Jackson at a salary of £91 a year. When he retired in 1845 as 'a man of great respectability', the then Governor, George Gipps, granted him an annual retirement pension of £182, with which he bought a run-down bar in George Street and turned it into an inn, the Steam Packet, which he ran with his wife Elizabeth, a widow whom he had been given permission to marry in 1818.

As for his cottage – four subsequent government coxswains lived in it until 1845, when it became the headquarters of Sydney Water Police. In 1864 it became a Sailors' Home, and after restoration and archaeological investigation now serves as Sydney Harbour National Park's information centre.

3 110 George Street North, The Rocks

Cadman's Cottage

THE RUM HOSPITAL

The New South Wales Parliament House and the Mint Museum occupy what remains of the 'Rum Hospital', erected in 1816 by a consortium of businessmen using convict labour and expecting to recover their costs from a monopoly on rum imports granted to them by Governor Lachlan Macquarie, to whom the British Government had denied funds for a hospital.

When the convict architect Francis Greenway inspected the builders' work he was appalled: the foundations were meagre, the stonework was already disintegrating, and he asserted that the building 'must soon fall into ruin'. He supervised repairs, but even in 1980, when restoration was undertaken, unsuspected weaknesses in the structure were still to be found.

Part of the north wing of the hospital first held a temporary courthouse, and then became surgeons' quarters. In the nineteenth century the Legislative Council took it over. The south wing was planned as quarters for the Assistant Surgeon, but instead housed hospital wards and was proposed as a military hospital. It was used as a dispensary for the poor before, in 1854, becoming the Sydney branch of the Royal Mint.

The Rum Hospital is the oldest public building in Sydney, though not the first hospital. This was in a series of tents set up the day after Governor Arthur Phillip landed with the First Fleet. Then a prefabricated building arrived from England, and was erected near what is now Nurses' Walk, in the Rocks. Governor Macquarie's solution to the British Parliament's parsimony was ingenious, though it led to much argument and bad feeling. The Governor himself appears to have had a hand in the building's design, together with a John O'Hearden (who signed himself as architect, but of whom nothing else is apparently known).

Paths under the Riverside Expressway

The building was an ambitious one for a settlement which was still in its infancy, and parts of it were always used by bodies unconnected with medicine. The contentious Supreme Court Judge, Jeffrey Hart Bent, irritably assented to part of the north wing being used as a temporary courthouse, violently disliking his neighbour in the building, surgeon D'Arcy Wentworth. Meanwhile the sick of two regiments stationed in Sydney were cared for in the south wing, while the town's Store Master worked upstairs. The Sydney Dispensary, providing free treatment for 'poor persons', took over the south wing in 1845, until it moved into the central section of the hospital. The interior of this wing was considerably altered when the Mint moved in; it housed the Mint Museum for a time before becoming the home of the Historic Houses Trust.

But what of the hub of the hospital? In 1879 the jerry-building of the original structure came home to roost, and the central block had to be demolished. There was a competition for a new design, won by architect Thomas Rowe, who so underestimated his costs that work came to a standstill and was only completed in 1894, with three sandstone buildings by John Kirkpatrick. Meanwhile nursing training went on in the Nightingale wing, built to Florence Nightingale's specifications; the Italianate courtyard with its elaborate fountain is one of the most elegant parts of the building.

The whole ménage was restored during the 1980s, and many tourists may well pass it by without realizing its age, or that it continues to house the oldest legislative body in Australia. Most, however, will stop to rub the nose of the handsome replica of the Florentine boar which stands outside to receive donations to hospital funds.

 Macquarie Street, Sydney

MACQUARIE PLACE

Governor Arthur Phillip and the first settlers gave little thought to the idea of public parks; early Sydney was a jumble of houses only vaguely conforming to any kind of plan. But as it turned out, an open space materialised between the first Government House (and the houses of other officers), the Tank Stream, and the stores and warehouses of what became Circular Quay.

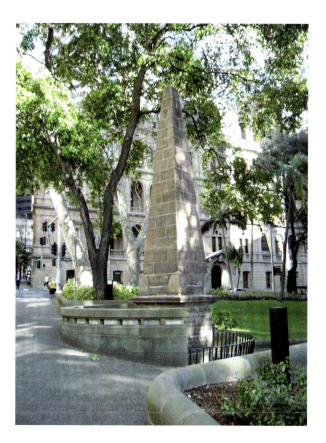

It was in the centre of this space that in 1818 Governor Lachlan Macquarie paid one Edward Cureton to mount an obelisk from which, he ordained, all distances between Sydney and elsewhere in the colony should be measured. The establishment of the space as a public park was underlined the following year, when it was enclosed by a low sandstone wall and an iron fence, and a sandstone Doric fountain was set up in its centre. A second tie to Governor Phillip and the first fleet is the large anchor mounted on a plinth at the north side of the park: this is the anchor of HMS Sirius, Phillip's flagship, recovered from the site of its wreck at Norfolk Island.

Macquarie Place is considerably smaller than it once was. When Circular Quay was built, between 1839 and 1847, a large section of it was swallowed by surrounding streets so that the obelisk, once in the middle, is now on the eastern side, near what was once a pretty 1807 small underground men's lavatory with a glass dome and art nouveau ironwork over the entrance. This has now been filled in – though with sand, which in theory could be removed (a desirable ambition).

Nearby is an equally delightful 1870 drinking fountain with an ornate iron canopy, bearing the injunction KEEP THE PAVEMENT DRY. Seven of these were ordered from Macfarlane's of Scotland in 1870; the other six have vanished. What by all accounts was the handsome Doric fountain dedicated to Governor Macquarie was demolished in 1883 to make way for a large, imposing, entirely uninteresting statue of the now forgotten Thomas Sutcliffe Mort, an auctioneer, financier and leading protagonist of frozen meat exports.

The neighbourhood has lively cafés and bars; otherwise this is a gentle and relaxed area, shaded by two splendid Moreton Bay figs, and two plane trees.

5 Corner of Bridge and Loftus Streets, Circular Quay

Macquarie Place

MACQUARIE'S LIGHTHOUSE

Until 1818 bonfires were lit on the South Head to guide shipping. During the long months while the first Australians almost starved to death, Governor Philip set up a flagstaff at South Head, from which midshipman Daniel Southwell kept a desperate daily watch. Later, when ships did begin to arrive, the Governor ordered a beacon whose fitful light was for a quarter of a century the only guide at night for mariners seeking the entrance to Port Jackson.

Governor Lachlan Macquarie then commissioned the convict architect Francis Greenway to design and build a lighthouse which, when it was completed, he described as 'a noble magnificent edifice'. Its light shone out over twenty miles of sea, the oil-burning lamps flashing every minute from a revolving cradle powered by clockwork and carefully maintained by Australia's first lighthouse keeper, Robert Watson, who had reached Australia with the First Fleet as quartermaster of the Sirius.

That first building stood for sixty years, but as Greenway had warned Macquarie the sandstone gradually crumbled and began to fall away, so that iron bands had to be placed around the lighthouse to secure it. In 1878 it became clear that the whole edifice was likely to collapse, and it was condemned as unsafe. The architect James Barnet carefully replicated the original design, and for a brief while the two lighthouses stood together – Barnet's carefully aligned so that mariners would not be misled by a sudden change in the position of the light.

While the Macquarie Lighthouse was Australia's first, Barnet's was naturally the more efficient – indeed its builder described it as the most efficient in the world, with a giant lens and an electric light. This was the cause of a tremendous row between Barnet and the Superintendent of Electric Telegraphs, who had serious doubts whether an architect could be expected to know anything about the complicated behaviour of electricity. However, Barnet electrocuted no-one, and went on to employ another original notion – the revolving mechanism worked by gas rather than steam, 'for reasons of cleanliness, economy, freedom from dust, smoke, etc'.

The new lighthouse was much admired, with its ornate decoration, and the crowned head of a placid Queen Victoria presiding over the main entrance. Barnet went on to design many other Australian lighthouses, but none more significant than his replica of Macquarie's.

6 Corner of Old South Head and Macquarie Road, Vaucluse

HYDE PARK BARRACKS

On May 20, 1819, Governor Lachlan Macquarie gave a feast for the convicts who had just been marched into the new barracks specially built for them at the north end of Hyde Park, which he proudly described as 'the best and most complete in any of His Majesty's foreign dominions'. The barracks was the first official accommodation built for the convicts, who had previously boarded with whoever would take them, or lived rough in the Rocks, where they had formed into violent bands of thieves to terrify the law-abiding.

Macquarie took the opportunity to grant the architect of the barracks, Francis Greenway, an absolute pardon. Greenway had arrived in Sydney in 1814, his sentence of death for forgery commuted to transportation for fourteen years. He had been an architect practising in Bristol, and with Macquarie's backing was soon at work in Sydney, where he gave advice on the building of the Rum Hospital (see p.30) and designed the Macquarie Lighthouse on the south head of the harbour (p.42). He was also to design churches in Sydney, Liverpool and Windsor, St Matthews' Anglican Church at Windsor being his masterpiece.

Macquarie had considerable difficulty in realising his plans for making Sydney a handsome city with buildings that matched its growing self-confidence. From the moment he stepped ashore as Governor in December 1809 he faced criticism of overspending from his masters in London. Within three months he was insisting that a barracks and a general hospital were 'an absolute necessity', while there must also eventually be court and administrative buildings. The English Government's response was that he was to practise the strictest economy in order to 'lessen the charge of the colony to the Mother Country'. But the Governor had already ordered work to start on the Hyde Park Barracks, to be followed promptly by a military hospital, a records office and a house for the colony's chaplain – 'all which are absolutely indispensable'.

Francis Greenway

> Greenway's design for the barracks provided a handsome building with accommodation for about six hundred male convicts, who slept in hammocks in twelve large rooms. An increased population of convicts raised the number of inhabitants to fourteen hundred, on occasion. Smaller outbuildings housed the deputy superintendent and his staff – kitchen, bakery, mess rooms and privies.

Convict accommodation elsewhere freed the barracks for use as an immigration depot for single women, and after thirty years hammocks gave way to iron bedsteads. The respectable ladies of Sydney came to observe and interview the inhabitants for possible use as domestic servants, while over the following years the outbuildings became offices and workplaces for the Government Printer, the district courts, the Rifle Corps and other institutions.

In 1862 the third floor of the main building became home for three hundred and more elderly homeless women. Between 1887 and 1979 the barracks was used for various purposes, including The Marine Court, the offices of the Weights and Measures department and the Master in Lunacy. Demolition was threatened in the early twentieth century, but against odds the building was saved and is now a museum with an emphasis on convict history.

Greenway went on to design more than forty buildings, of which eleven remain standing. Sadly, he died in poverty, but the Barracks, together with St James' Church, standing opposite, and the old Supreme Court building make a group which remain an indication of the civic centre which Governor Macquarie envisaged – a tribute to Greenway's vision and the Governor's firm belief that Sydney should become a handsome, as well as a prosperous, city.

Queens Square, Macquarie Street, Sydney

ST JAMES' CHURCH

The oldest church building in Sydney, St James' was originally planned by Governor Lachlan Macquarie as a courthouse – part of a grand civic square at the centre of the town. However, the visiting Commissioner of Enquiry, J. T. Bigge, sent to Sydney with sweeping powers to overrule the Governor's ambitious plans for the colony, insisted that the building should be completed as a church. The former convict Francis Greenway (now Civil Architect) had designed the building, and in January 1822 convicts from the Hyde Park Barracks, across the way, attended an unofficial service in the unfinished church, which was consecrated two years later.

St James' was very much a church of its time, with high box pews rented to the gentry, and benches for the less affluent and the downright poor. The respectable part of the congregation entered by the north porch; convicts came in under the tower and climbed to the gallery, which they shared with the military. Galleries were enlarged as the church became ever more fashionable and well attended.

Set on sandstone foundations, St James' is made of brick, and chimes well with the Barracks and the remains of the Rum Hospital. For generations it was loved and well attended. But it remained close to traditional Anglican custom and usage in the face of the growing evangelical movement of the mid-nineteenth century, and its congregation began to shrink as suburban Sydney acquired its own churches. St James' seemed increasingly antique – not only in its ecclesiastical practises but in its furnishings; modern Gothic churches elsewhere were more fashionable and better attended. Changes became inevitable, and the interior as we see it now is not as Greenway planned it, for as in England the Victorians indulged in a comprehensive fit of church restoration. St James' was attacked in 1900 and comprehensively remodelled by J. H. Buckeridge, who added a chancel and apse (where the organ was placed) and virtually stripped the interior bare, ripping out the old furniture and installing new bench pews. Happily he stopped short of removing

the many memorial tablets and carvings which had been placed on the walls over the years, some of which commemorate the early explorers of the continent, while others have often elaborate stories to tell of adventure and mishap.

The preaching and devoutly elaborate services of the Anglo-Catholic Isaac Carr Smith, appointed to the church in 1895, turned St James' into what for the time was a very High Church indeed, appealing to a section of society to which ostentatious low-church Puritanism was anathema. The result was a growing congregation travelling into the centre of Sydney especially to attend Smith's services.

Below the street level of St James' there is a large undercroft with handsome brick vaulting, which for over a century served as home to the church's vergers. It then became a school, and after the reconstruction of 1900 provided parish offices. It is worth visiting for the murals painted in one of the bays in 1929 by members of the Turramurra artists' community – three ships, as in the traditional carol, come sailing into Port Jackson, with the Harbour Bridge half-built.

Incidentally, Commissioner Bigge's insistence that Macquarie's courthouse should become a church may be explained by the fact that when he returned to England his brother-in-law, a wine-merchant, swiftly took holy orders and was immediately appointed Archdeacon of Sydney, with the fine new church at his disposal.

8 173 King Street, Sydney

DON BANK

The oldest house in North Sydney, now known as Don Bank, started life as St Leonard's Cottage. There was a house on the site in 1823, part of Crows Nest Farm, and the present one may well be the only surviving example in Sydney of an Australian slab-walled house.

The construction of the original four-room cottage was basic: four posts were driven into the ground and two beams were placed, one on the ground and the other at head-height. Between grooves in these beams vertical slabs of cedar made the walls, the spaces between the slabs filled with clay to keep out the weather. The roof was originally made of saplings to which sheets of bark were tied. Later corrugated iron covered it, one of many changes, including the addition of several rooms.

The interior decoration also of course changed over the years, but the colour and style of wallpapers and paint has been researched and painstakingly reproduced, while original floors, fabrics and window fittings can still be seen in some of the rooms. In the garden, a few old plants survive – most notably a splendid magnolia.

The advertisement in the Sydney Morning Herald on 20 October 1854 offering the cottage for sale describes it as 'beautifully finished, all the rooms papered' (some of the original wallpaper has been found and preserved) 'commanding picturesque views of the waters of Port Jackson and its numerous bays and headlands'. While at that time residents would walk down a bushy track to the water's edge to be rowed across the harbour, the advertisement pointed out that it was now certain that a bridge across the harbour would soon place Crows Nest within minutes of the centre of town. The inhabitants of Don Bank would actually have to wait another eighty years for that!

There has been much coming and going in the house over the last century and a half. In the late 1850s, the owner was Robert Thomson and his wife – Robert did much to establish the insurance industry in Australia. Then in the 1870s, after he had retired from sea, came Captain Benjamin Jenkins, late captain of the John Knox, (he was to become Mayor of St Leonard's), then a dentist, two saddlers …

By 1903 the house was almost derelict, but it was eventually restored and cared for by loving owners until in 1978 the newly formed Heritage Act assisted in its preservation. Carefully restored, it is now open to the public.

9 6 Napier Street, North Sydney

VAUCLUSE HOUSE

Vaucluse House is one of the relatively few great houses of Australia to have survived almost complete within its original setting. It could be transferred to the English home counties without appearing bizarre; its crenellated parapets and turrets resemble those with which many Victorian families with social aspirations decorated their houses 'at home'. William Charles Wentworth (the barrister, author, explorer and publisher of The Australian newspaper) who bought Vaucluse in 1827 and turned it from a cottage into a house, was, however, the illegitimate son of a convict woman, and thus uninfluenced by any personal memories of English Victorian mansions.

The first building on the site was built by a convict, Sir Henry Browne Hayes, who abducted an extremely rich young English heiress, was sentenced to death, then transported rather than hanged. He surprisingly named his little house after the French estate of the Italian poet Petrarch. That was in 1803; almost a quarter of a century later Wentworth bought the land, swept away the cottage, and built his own house.

Despite the fact that the parapets and turrets seem wildly inappropriate when matched with the graceful appearance of the large bay window and louvered shutters of the drawing room, giving onto a front verandah with slender Gothic revival posts, the combination somehow works, and the house is one of the most delightful in the state, if not the country. A charming feature is the little colonnaded Italianate courtyard between the kitchen and the entry hall of the house itself. But gracefulness runs with utility; signs that this was a gentleman's house with every convenience not only include the large kitchen with its attendant larder and dairy, but the adjoining butler's pantry and housekeeper's room and the cellar, reached by an outside staircase, with one room for storing food and another with brick-built wine bins.

The use of some of the rooms has naturally changed over the years, and some were added from time to time. A breakfast room and small tea-room joined the dining room, for instance; but the large drawing-room remains as it was when the house was new-built, at the front, overlooking the garden and single-storeyed. The bedrooms are above the rear part of the house, rising to a second storey. A pump from a reservoir in the courtyard once sent water up to the bathroom in the bedroom wing, but with a charming eccentricity there is another bathroom on the ground floor, where a door from the terrace gives into a room with a black-and-white tiled plunge-pool, and a wire with an ingenious system of pullies which was no doubt installed to summon a servant with warm towels before the bather braved the open air to return to the house.

Wentworth, having supervised the building of the turrets, the kitchen wing and nearby stables, took his family to Europe in 1853, returning nine years later to set another series of alterations and additions in train – new Gothic-revival columns to the balcony, a fountain in the middle of the front lawn, and many new features in the gardens. After his death, the Wentworth family continued to care for the house until 1900; ten years later a trust was established to maintain it and the house was opened to the public. The Historic Houses Trust took over responsibility for the property in 1981.

10 Wentworth Road, Vaucluse

Vaucluse House

JUNIPER HALL

Comfortable solidity are the words that come to mind when visiting Juniper Hall, the epitome of a wealthy man's middle-class metropolitan mansion in the Australian Georgian style. It was built by the former convict Robert Cooper, who arrived in Sydney in 1813 having been transported for receiving stolen goods.

Pardoned after five years, he made a fortune distilling gin. It seems probable that he designed the house himself, for his third wife Sarah and a large family of children, who moved in in 1828. He claimed it as 'the finest house in Sydney'; the spacious rooms ranged around a central staircase, the bedrooms at the back giving onto a generous balcony with a view over Port Jackson from the then almost unoccupied hilltop. During the nineteenth century a row of shops was built in the front garden, obscuring the house from Oxford Street. Taking responsibility for the property, the National Trust has demolished these, and the house now displays its impressive façade to the street.

Juniper Hall must have provoked much admiration and envy when it first rose in the relatively new area of Paddington. Its well-balanced appearance, with the unusual feature of an upstairs balcony (to say nothing of the capacious cellar), was among the most impressive of its time. Named because its very existence depended on Cooper's devotion to the juniper berry (his gin was the first to be distilled in Sydney), the house was not occupied by its builder for long. Short of money by 1831, he let the building to the Attorney General, John Kinchela, who promptly re-named it Ormond Hall. Later it was leased to the Society for the Relief of Destitute Children, and became an orphanage. Cooper went bankrupt eighteen years later – but had cannily placed the hall in his wife's name – and the family continued to own it until 1877, when it was sold to the government. Within the next decade considerable alterations were made, though the details of these remain obscure. In 1924 it was sold to an owner who intended to demolish it. He was prevented, and the National Trust, now the

owners, intended it for a Museum of Childhood – a venture which unfortunately failed. Juniper Hall is currently tenanted by an antique dealer and managed by the National Trust.

11 250 Oxford Street, Paddington

THE QUARANTINE STATION

In 1828 Governor Darling's son died from whooping cough, and as a direct result the Governor decided that the colony needed a secure quarantine station. Hearing that there were sick convicts on board the transport Busserah Merchant he ordered her to anchor at Spring Cove, and her entire crew and the convicts and guards were landed and housed in tents on shore. From that time North Head was used for quarantine, and ten years later permanent buildings were established there on 'healthy ground' and 'sick ground' to separate the infected from the healthy.

There was a special building – a so-called parlatorio – in which visitors could talk to their quarantined friends (for the station served migrants as well as convicts) and another where mail could be fumigated. The fairly basic station served well enough until the outbreak of smallpox in 1881, when facilities were overhauled and extended. Today many of the original buildings remain, including the bath houses where passengers were disinfected (cubicles for the well-to-do, rows of showers for the less affluent), close supervision ensuring that no-one escaped disinfection.

The quarantine station is often referred to as the most haunted place in Sydney, and certainly it is not difficult to be affected by the stories of the separation of families and the death of loved ones which distressed both the convicts landed there in the early days and the victims of the smallpox epidemic. Fifty of the smallpox victims were later brought here for burial. But there are also social implications: the careful separation of first – and third-class passengers, for instance. The passengers' luggage was carried up-hill by a special tramway to the nicely designed cottages in which first class were housed, while others enjoyed much more basic amenities. For many people their time at the station was almost a holiday; for others something like imprisonment. Perhaps the most telling of the buildings is the

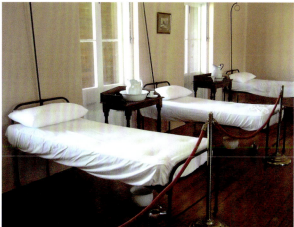

The Quarantine Station

remaining first-class bathhouse, with an uneasy resemblance to those at concentration camps. But there is much to admire – the hospital, the laundry where over fifty cement washing tubs could wash the linen from a whole ship within twenty-four hours, and the fumigating room where Fraser's Disinfecting Apparatus and Lyons Patent Steam Disinfector ensured that every article brought into Sydney via the station was free from infection. Between 1828 and 1984 over 580 vessels were quarantined in Spring Cove and more than 13,000 people quarantined in the facilities; some 572 were buried in three burial grounds on the hillside.

Today the Quarantine Station is a privately-operated conference centre that has been renamed 'Q Station' but parts are still open to the public, with evening ghost tours and an education centre that showcases the history of this remarkable site. The Boilerhouse Restaurant is named after its location within the restored boiler-house whence steam was sent to the autoclaves and boiling water to the showers and laundry.

 North Head Scenic Drive, Manly

TWO SCHOOLS: SYDNEY GRAMMAR SCHOOL, CLEVELAND STREET PUBLIC SCHOOL

Sydney College – now Sydney Grammar School – was founded in 1830, and the following year took possession of the 'Big School', a building in Hyde Park designed by Edward Hallen, later architect of the Argyle Cut. The 'Big School' still stands, with extensions built in 1856 and 1857 by Edmund Blacket, architect of the main buildings of Sydney University. In 1876 there was another extension, and some earlier buildings were demolished – as, later, was the fine double stair in the north wing. The appropriate portico was added as recently as 1952.

In 1825 Laurence Hynes Halloran, who had fled from England to escape his debtors, awarded himself a degree in Divinity and opened a 'public free grammar school' which eventually metamorphosed into Sydney College, taken over in 1853 by the University of Sydney. An Act of Parliament established the Grammar School as a result of complaints about the low educational standard of University undergraduates. The Grammar School buildings range from Big School to the later Blacket buildings on each side of it, the somewhat nondescript Palladium Building, and the Stanley Street buildings which include one 1867 cottage still used as a classroom. The multi-storey modern buildings make the best use of a small land area.

Cleveland Street School was one of four 'model schools' erected as a result of the Gold Rush of the 1850s, which had resulted in a 'baby boom'. It first housed 215 students in prefabricated galvanised iron buildings, but in 1867 new buildings were designed and erected by the architect G. A. Mansfield, who also designed many other prominent Sydney buildings. His school, which cost a generous £6,397, was described in the press as 'a palace'. There were originally three schoolrooms: one for boys, one for girls and one for infants.

Cleveland Strret School

The Gothic Revival buildings of Cleveland Street School – now Cleveland Street Intensive English High School – were remarkably elaborate for their purpose, but were also carefully utilitarian. The small windows of the three classrooms were placed sufficiently high up to make idle window-gazing impossible for the students, and, unlike many school buildings of the time, making provision for heating – open fireplaces, with a coal allowance supervised by the teachers. In 1891 £4,399 was spent on a new wing designed in a style which its architect, W. E. Kemp, described as 'Moderated Romanesque'. At the same time the City Council gave permission for pupils to use Prince Albert Road as a playground (Mansfield not having thought to provide such an amenity). In 1909, when 2,144 boys and girls were enrolled, yet another wing was added, with classrooms described as 'shops'; another, extremely unhandsome, appeared in 1924, and a fourth in 1968.

The high school moved out in 1977 to the adjacent suburb of Alexandria. The buildings at Cleveland Street became an annex to the new high school and the Cleveland Street Intensive English Centre (which is what the old high school buildings are now called) now provides tuition in English, and is also used by community groups.

13 Sydney Grammar School, College Street, Darlinghurst

13 Cleveland Street Intensive English High School, Corner of Cleveland and Chalmers Streets Surry Hills

Sydney Grammer School

EXPERIMENT FARM COTTAGE

In 1789 Australia's first Governor, Arthur Phillip, granted a former convict, Cornishman James Ruse, thirty acres of land at Parramatta, hoping that he might be able to cultivate it sufficiently to provide food and shelter for his family. Within a year this first experiment in self-sufficiency was a success, and Ruse was given another thirty acres.

Experiment Farm Cottage stands probably not far from Ruse's own house on land purchased from him by Surgeon John Harris. Built in the 1830s – and thus one of Australia's earliest buildings – it resembles one of the small houses which Harris would have seen during his service in colonial India. It has a neat, unostentatious façade, with a pretty fanlight above the front door and a balcony to shelter against the heat. French doors can be opened to allow air into the front rooms, which remain as they were first built, nicely proportioned and with neat cedar chimney-pieces. It is probable that originally one was a living and dining room, with steps leading down to a garden, and the other the main bedroom.

Surgeon Harris never actually lived at Experiment Farm Cottage – he had a large house at Ultimo – but it was certainly part of Harris Farm, comprising over three hundred acres of what he called 'barren unhospitable territory'. He died in 1838, and the cottage was then taken by the Colonial Treasurer, one Pieter Laurentz Campbell, until Harris's descendants took it over. They were in various ways unsuccessful in maintaining it, and in 1903 Alexander Fraser became a tenant. An enthusiastic photographer he left interesting records of the house, his family and the area.

In 1921 the Harris family sold the cottage: the National Trust accepted it in 1961, finding it necessary to do repairs which involved changes to the structure. Later, some of these were reversed – concrete was removed from the stone flagging of the verandah, and original colour schemes restored. Most ambitiously, by 2001, in a splendid tribute to Australia's care for its heritage, nearby houses were demolished and a road re-routed so that the original carriage-way and grounds could be restored to their probable original appearance.

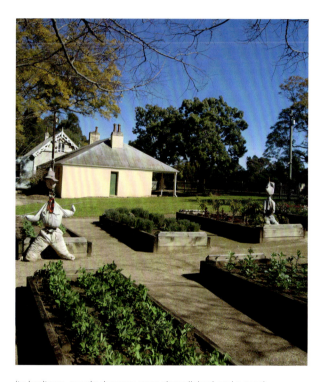

14 9 Ruse St, Harris Park

POTTS POINT

Heartened and encouraged by the success of the 'green bans' (see p.22) the residents of Victoria Street, Potts Point, determined to fight the plans put forward in the 1970s to demolish most of their houses and replace them with high-rise apartment and office blocks. Their success resulted in the preservation of a delightful street of typical 19th century terrace houses (with the exception of a few bizarrely obtrusive high-rise buildings).

However the campaign had a cost: Juanita Nielsen, the publisher of the local newspaper which led the protests, disappeared without trace in July 1975; an inquest returned an open verdict, but there is local conviction that she died for the cause.

Terraces like those in Victoria Street arose in Potts Point and elsewhere when large estates were subdivided, and builders saw the advantage of constructing rows of houses sharing common walls. With stucco façades and lacy cast-iron balustrades they graced streets which became almost boulevards, with small well-kept gardens shaded by trees. By the 1890s more moderately well-off Sydneysiders lived in such terrace houses than in any other form of accommodation.

In 1831 it was required that houses built at Potts Point (formerly known as Woolloomooloo Hill) should cost not less than a thousand pounds to build, must all face the city, and be approved by the then Governor. This resulted in an area where such relatively modest but handsome terraces as those in Victoria Street are interspersed with large, handsome Regency-style mansions such as Rockwall House (advertised as 'a splendid Italian villa') with its striking verandah, and its twin, Tusculum, in Manning Street. Both these buildings became derelict in the 1970s, but were happily rescued. Elizabeth Bay House, in Onslow Avenue, is an example of an earlier style – its domed oval saloon and handsome sweeping staircase, built in the 1830s, are part of one of the finest colonial interiors in Sydney.

In the twentieth century the area saw some of the first apartment buildings to be erected in the city, and there are probably more Art Deco buildings in Potts Point than in any other part of Sydney – three striking apartment buildings in Macleay Street, for instance. Happily, the relatively recent passion for Art Deco suggests that these and others will be preserved with the same passion as has conserved earlier buildings.

Empire Hotel, Potts Point

DARLINGHURST GAOL

A substantial new gaol for the colony was planned in the 1820s, the design by Mortimer William Lewis, an Englishman who later became Colonial Architect. He is said to have based it on a prison in Philadelphia, on the later frequently-used notion of buildings radiating out from a central chapel. The prisoners themselves cut the Sydney sandstone used to build their prison – convict markings can still be seen on the stones. The building was not fully completed until 1885, and was never completely satisfactory.

Built to hold 723 prisoners, 156 of them women, it was constantly overcrowded and there were continual problems with security. Buildings crowded together with little space between them meant that in summer the air became fetid and unhealthy, while there was never satisfactory sewage disposal – the authorities being reluctant to dig the necessary tunnels for fear they would be used as a means of escape. Sickness was endemic. Closed as a gaol in 1912, the building was briefly used to imprison 'enemy aliens' during the First World War, but then became a splendidly expansive national art college.

In 1841 a long line of convicts walked in their chains from their old gaol in George Street to the new buildings, where the Governor, Henry Keck, greeted them. He was an enterprising man who organised his charges into running a pig farm (the pigs fed on prisoners' rations), making clothing and boots for sale, and fishing (trustees were sent out to fish at Woolloomooloo at night) – all for his own profit. Prostitution – the most profitable business of all – was run from the women's' cells. Keck also formed a small prisoners' orchestra which played at local functions. In addition, he presided over public executions, held at a platform built above the main gate in Forbes Street. Hundreds, including children, gathered in the street below – on one occasion a crowd calculated to amount to as many as ten thousand was said to have watched the death of a particularly notorious murderer. Many other executions took place inside – the head gaoler

Darlinghurst Gaol

boasted that he could hang six prisoners comfortably, seven at a pinch. The most famous was probably the celebrated bushranger 'Captain Moonlight'.

The poet Henry Lawson, imprisoned for drunkenness and non-payment of alimony, left a portrait of 'Starvinghurst Gaol' in his poem entitled 'One Hundred and Three' (a reference to his prisoner number):

> *They shut a man in the four-by-eight,*
> *with a six-inch slit for air,*
>
> *Twenty-three hours of the twenty-four,*
> *to brood on his virtues there.*
>
> *And the dead stone walls and the iron door close*
> *in as an iron band*
>
> *On eyes that followed the distant haze*
> *far out on the level land . . .*
>
> *The great, round church with its volume of sound,*
> *where we dare not turn our eyes —*
>
> *They take us there from our separate hells*
> *to sing of Paradise . . .'*

In 1921 the NSW Department of Education adapted the building for use as the East Sydney Technical College, and the National Art School occupies the site. Although the last hanging took place in 1907, it is said that stains have been left in the atmosphere, with teachers and students complaining of regular hauntings of classrooms and staircases.

 Forbes Street, Darlinghurst.

ADMIRALTY HOUSE

In what is arguably the finest position overlooking Port Jackson, Admiralty House is the official residence of the Governor-General of Australia. It originated, in 1842-3, as a plain and elegant single-storey L-shaped house designed and built for himself by Lieut.-Colonel J. G. N. Gibbes, collector of customs in New South Wales. He named it Wotonga. It passed through several hands between 1851 and 1885, when it was purchased by the colonial government as a residence for the Admiral of the Navy. When the last British Admiral left Australia in 1913, Admiralty House (as it was now called) became the residence of the Governors-General.

In 1930, during the depression, Admiralty House was closed and its contents auctioned, Sir Isaac Isaacs becoming the first Governor-General to live permanently in Canberra. During the next six years it fell into desuetude, the rooms unfurnished and the gardens growing wild. In 1936 the state government re-opened it as the Sydney residence for the Governors-General, and it has been used for that purpose ever since, also serving to entertain distinguished visitors, including members of the Royal Family and the Pope.

Kirribilli Point was fortified against the Russians during the Crimean War, and an officer of the Royal Engineers was stationed in Wotonga to install a battery of five muzzle-loading guns overlooking the harbour. Next door, Kirribilli House was built, originally to house the Governor-General's staff but now the official residence of the Prime Minister. There is a tenuous connection with the Crown: Colonel Gibbes was reputed to be the illegitimate child of the Duke of York, second son of King George III.

In contrast to the slight blowsiness of the mock-Gothic Government House, Admiralty House has an air of quiet distinction – the elegant aunt, perhaps, of a somewhat over-assertive niece. The original house, Wotonga, still stands within the present building. A second storey was added in the first Admiral's day, as was the wide colonnaded verandah on the two sides facing the harbour. A covered Admiral's Walk once led to the waterside where his barge was berthed. The interior has been much changed, a grand double staircase now leading to the first floor from a slightly disproportionate but handsome hallway. The house is open to the public on one day every year.

 109 Kirribilli Avenue, Kirribilli

Admiralty House

GOVERNMENT HOUSE, SYDNEY

It seemed to Governor Sir Richard Bourke, in 1834, that no architect then working in Sydney had the talent or expertise necessary to design such an important building as the new Government House he was planning. He therefore sent to London, where the choice fell on Edward Blore, who had worked on the completion of Buckingham Palace and on other royal buildings.

A personal friend of Sir Walter Scott, Blore was fascinated by the architecture of Scottish baronial castles, and when his plans arrived they were for a Gothic revival imitation castle which matched Francis Greenway's crenulated Government stables, just down the road. Blore of course had little idea of the site chosen for his building, at Bennelong Point, and it was decided to turn his design around so that the entrance faced south while the main rooms looked over the garden to the harbour.

The building was generally approved; the reception rooms were considered as handsome as they were spacious, and a water closet of the newest and most efficient design had been installed for the comfort and convenience of royal guests.

The first Government House in Sydney was a canvas tent brought from England for the purpose and erected by Governor Arthur Phillip the day after he stepped ashore in January 1788. However, within three months he had laid the foundation of a more substantial building, which with alterations and additions served the colony for almost fifty years. In 1816 Governor Macquarie commissioned Greenway to build a new Government House; but as usual the British Government's lack of financial support – indeed, harsh criticisms of overspending – sank the scheme, and all that was completed was the stables (now, and for some years, the home of the Conservatorium of Music).

The colony was equally short of money when Bourke's plan was put forward, and it was not until 1843 that his successor, Sir George Gipps, was able to use some of the rooms for a ball in honour of Queen Victoria's twenty-fourth birthday. The building was finished four years later at a total cost of £46,000, which made it by far the most expensive building yet erected in New South Wales.

There was an instant jostling among the great and good of the city for invitations to Government House, the style of which had an almost immediate influence on the architecture of the city. The state rooms – drawing room, sitting room, and two-storey ballroom with a pleasant small balcony for an orchestra – were much admired. There was some juggling when it came to furnishings, financial constraint preventing a really uniform scheme. Some of the furniture was specially commissioned from local craftsmen, but more was collected from Old Government House at Parramatta, and some imported from Britain. Much of this remains.

Naturally, under twenty-seven Governors and their wives, there were modifications and additions. A porte-cochére was added in 1873, and in 1900 there were extensions to the main reception rooms. Rooms upstairs were used by the families of resident Governors, visiting royalty and other distinguished guests including Queen Elizabeth II, Prince Charles and Lady Diana. As early as 1900 there was some grumbling about the undue magnificence of the accommodation provided for English Governors, but it was not until 1996 that Government House ceased to be a residence, and was opened to the public. Entrance is free, though sometimes curtailed when official functions are held there, for the house is still used by the current Governor to receive honoured guests, to swear inGovernment Ministers, and for official receptions.

17 Royal Botanic Gardens, Macquarie Street, Sydney

Government House, Sydney

THE GARRISON CHURCH

After the early years of the colony, when simply staying alive took precedence over organised religion, attention turned to church building, and among the churches opened during the first half of the century was St Philip's in York Street, established in 1810 (though the present building dates from 1856). As Victorian values began to take hold of previously unregenerate Sydney, church attendance swelled, and in 1830 a body of respectable parishioners argued that a new church was needed to take the overflow from St Philip's. Bishop Broughton agreed, and the Rev. W. Cowper, minister of the parish, 'in a strain of fervent piety and unaffected simplicity', as he put it, suggested that the building should be dedicated to the Holy Trinity.

Almost immediately after the church's opening in 1843 it became associated with the garrison at nearby Dawes Point, and so was known less by its official name than simply as the 'Garrison Church', attended until 1870 by troops from most of the regiments stationed in Sydney, from the Royal West Kents and the King's Own to the Northumberland Fusiliers, the Devonshires, the Prince of Wales Volunteers, the West Yorkshires and the Royal Irish.

Holy Trinity is a simple church that might be transplanted without ado to any village in the English countryside. The nave represents the church as it was originally built – the stone quarried from the rock of nearby Argyle Street, considerably before the completion of the Argyle Cut. The windows were originally barred – perhaps there was some concern about the church's proximity to the still doubtfully respectable Rocks. It swiftly became well attended – not only by parishioners and the military, but by seamen (Bishop Broughton regarded it as 'the Mariners' Church') – and over the years there were many improvements, notably the installation of the east window, considered one of the best in Australia.

There were also plans for a tower and spire, prepared by the distinguished architect Edmund Blacket, who designed the University of Sydney buildings and St Andrew's Cathedral. Alas, the £9500 which this would cost was beyond the reach of the parishioners, and the church remains towerless. However, the church was considerably enlarged, with a vestry and chancel, and the building was finally completed in 1878.

The Garrison Church

During the first years of the twentieth century, the church's association with the military strengthened, and regular services for Army and Navy personnel began to be customary – not only for troops stationed in Sydney, but the crews of visiting naval ships. During the First World War over half of the church's Bible Class members served abroad, and a refurbished organ was dedicated to 'the soldiers of the parish who did not return from the Great War'. During the Second World War the Garrison Hall became an Emergency Hostel for troops on leave. In 1952 plaques were set up in the church showing the crests of the various regiments whose members have worshipped at Holy Trinity.

18 Lower Fort and Argyle Streets, Millers Point

SYDNEY OBSERVATORY

Sydney Observatory stands on the highest piece of land in the area, once known as Windmill Hill, later as Citadel Hill, then Flagstaff Hill (the building is on the site of a former windmill).

Work began on it in 1856, under architect Alexander Dawson, who designed the sandstone buildings in an Italianate villa style, much used at the time for commercial accommodation. On a time-ball tower a ball dropped promptly each day at 1 pm. Formerly a cannon was fired nearby and at Fort Denison – a time-check for mariners' chronometes and residents. There were two observation rooms with telescopes, and offices and accommodation for an astronomer and his family. Later a library was added, and another telescope room. Astronomer Henry Chamberlain Russell – who served for a quarter of a century from 1870 – mapped the sky and began the publication of weather maps in the Sydney newspapers.

The present Observatory building was not the earliest. Out with the First Fleet came Second Lieut. William Dawes, charged by the Astronomer Royal to observe a comet which was expected to appear during the voyage. A widely popular young man, he set up an observatory and made various observations, particularly to establish the longitude of Sydney from Greenwich, to improve navigation. He also attempted to learn the language of the local Aborigines, and argued that this was his chief reason for taking an aboriginal mistress.

After Dawes returned to England in 1791 his observatory was neglected, and Governor King ordered the building in 1803 of Fort Philip as a defence against mutinous convicts; it never fired a shot in anger, and later became an important signal station, recording the arrival of ships in the harbour. It was Governor William Denison who chose it as the obvious place for a properly designed observatory, and Government astronomer William Scott began work there in 1858.

Observations were taken from the domed chamber which held the equatorial telescope and from a room with long, narrow windows suitable for the transit telescope. It was Scott's successor, Russell, who built the reputation of the Observatory and made its presence and work known throughout the world, taking very early astronomical photographs and participating in a major international programme to chart the entire sky.

As with so many Sydney institutions, questions arose with Federation in 1901, when the Federal Government took over responsibility for meteorological observation and forecasting, leaving the state of New South Wales to continue with astronomical observations with limited resources and lacking a dark-sky observation site. Science was also being nationalised and funding was made available for large telescopes in new observatories supported by the Federal Government. In the mean time Sydney Observatory astronomers continued work on the great Astrographic Catalogue: after 80 years, 53 volumes completed the Sydney section of the atlas.

The building was used for research for over 130 years; in 1982 it became a public observatory and astronomy education and heritage centre. The telescopes are still used by guides showing the public how the Observatory functioned, and the work it did. There is also a modern telescope.

In 1982 the Observatory became part of what is now the Powerhouse Museum, and plays a valuable part in education and the popularisation of astronomy, viewing stars, planets, the Moon and nebulae through telescopes every evening. It holds special events for eclipses, transit and other astronomical phenomena.

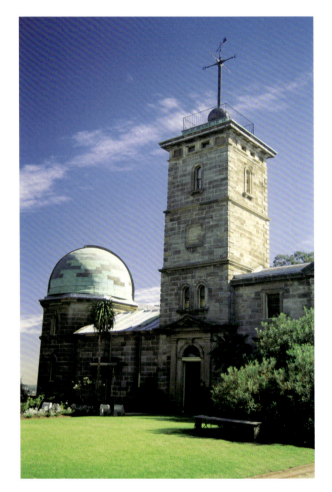

19 Watson Road, Observatory Hill, The Rocks

THE WATER POLICE COURT

The justices of Sydney were as convinced as those in Europe that official law offices should be sufficiently imposing to intimidate malefactors. When it was decided to build an office for the water police, Edmund Blacket was chosen to design it. Blacket, the English architect, had already designed six Australian churches, including the striking and much admired St Philip's, Sydney. He produced a building with an imposing façade and colonnaded portico, all in sandstone quarried from Bennelong Point.

The chosen site was at the corner of Phillip and Alfred streets, within a step of Circular Quay. The police station, with its charge room, offices and cells with weighty iron doors, was completed by 1856. The following year a second architect, Alexander Dawson, added more cells, offices and domestic quarters for the Water Police, and thirty years later another prominent Sydney architect, James Barnet – a Scot who had already designed the Sydney GPO and the Colonial Secretary's Building – built a magistrates' courthouse perfectly married to his predecessor's work and a second extremely handsome police station in George Street.

As with almost every other public building erected in Sydney in the nineteenth century, the building of the Water Police Court was delayed by lack of funds and lack of labour – so many artisans and workmen had joined the gold rush of the early 1850s, and prices had risen so dramatically, that the £4000 set aside for the work was completely inadequate to secure labour and complete the construction. It was eventually opened in 1856, and Mr Hutchinson Hothersal Brown, the Water Police Magistrate, moved in with his staff.

Two years later the Water Police moved from their cramped quarters in Cadman's Cottage to the Water Police Station, where they enjoyed the use of a kitchen and exercise yard, and there was accommodation upstairs for four policemen and their families.

This was opened in 1857, designed by Dawson, who the previous year had been appointed Colonial Architect in Sydney. He had previously been working in Tasmania, where he had built among other things a number of lighthouses and abattoirs, lunatic asylums and bridges, and several gaols. He later designed the Sydney Observatory.

In 1913 the Water Police moved into new accommodation at Dawes Point, and the Phillip Street building became a general police station. When the motor car became a serious object of police attention, the station became the home of a special police court for hearing traffic offences. In 1917 the Police Traffic Branch took up residence, and from 1926 onward all cases of traffic and parking offences committed in Sydney were heard in the court, although matters concerned with shipping and others which arose as the result of Water Police work were also heard here. In 1990 it was vacated by the police and the Historic Houses Trust took over responsibility for the building, which now houses the Justice and Police Museum.

4-8 Phillip Street, Sydney

ANDREW BOY CHARLTON POOL

One of Governor Macquarie's first acts when he reached Sydney in 1810 was to put a stop to the habit of men and boys stripping naked to bathe from the wharves. The cool waters of Port Jackson had been used by men to wash themselves for as long as humans had decided it was hygienic occasionally to do so; and of course, especially in the heat of summer, swimming was agreeable. Public nudity was however contrary to civilized European opinion – it was bracketed in the official mind with all sorts of other 'immoral and illicit intercourse' – a scandal to religion and decency.

The men and boys of Sydney had a simple answer to the inhibition: they took themselves off around the coast to less inhabited areas, where rocks and bushes protected them from the gaze of those likely to be offended. The most popular was the nearest – at the Fig Tree at Woolloomooloo, a place which became more and more popular after Mrs Macquarie's road was built in 1815 and made it easier to reach.

By 1825 the Fig Tree was the most popular bathing place in Sydney, with an abandoned hulk, the Ben Bolt, protecting the southern side of it. When the law made nude bathing dangerously susceptible to prosecution, a second hulk later provided shelter for changing and made it possible for women to use the bathing place. The Fig Tree was soon merely the most popular of a number of semi-official bathing places in the area and in 1858 the City Council demolished the last fragments of the hulks, and built Corporation Baths, still known as the Fig Tree Baths.

Their popularity was too great to resist change. In 1908 a new pool opened – the Domain Baths, known as 'the Dom,' with a 1700-seat grandstand. The growing popularity of competitive swimming made it a centre for record attempts. When in 1924 Andrew 'Boy' Charlton broke one Australian and two world records in one day, the pool inevitably became known by his name – officially so when an Olympic-sized pool opened in 1955. Poor design made this unpopular, and there was general pleasure when concrete cancer prompted its demolition. Public opinion insisted on a new complex on the original site. Costing over $10 million, it opened in 2002.

(21) 1c Mrs Macquaries Road, The Domain

MORTUARY TEMPLE

Leaving the centre of Sydney by Regent Street, unaware drivers may be surprised to see, on their left, what appears to be the entrance to a Victorian château, its Gothic porte-cochère ready to welcome one, perhaps, to an enjoyable weekend. Somehow, however, there seems something not quite right about the notion; and anyone entering would indeed find empty railway tracks passing alongside a platform and a row of nine handsome, elaborate arches. This is clearly no conventional entrance hall – at least for the living.

The building is in fact a Mortuary Temple, whose purpose was to give a properly solemn passage, in the 1860s, to a funeral party accompanying a coffin on its journey by train to the recently opened Necropolis – a spacious new cemetery at Rookwood (or Haslams Creek Cemetery, as it was then called). The Temple was designed by the celebrated architect James Barnet, whose major work included the General Post Office and the Customs House.

He also designed a receiving Temple at Rookwood, which was dismantled some years ago and transferred, stone by stone, to Ainslie, Canberra, where it is used as a chapel. Though the Redfern Mortuary Temple was restored in 1985, it is again in danger of dereliction, and has been closed to the public for some years.

It was the colonial government which commissioned the building of the Mortuary Temples to serve the Necropolis, which itself had been created in 1862 to solve the problem of overcrowding in city centre cemeteries. Trains began running from the Mortuary Temple in 1865, stopping at intermediate stations to pick up additional mourners and coffins. There were two types of hearse carriages, one of which held ten coffins on shelves which opened to allow access to and from the platforms. The second held up

to thirty coffins. The trains ran until 1948, when motor hearses became a more convenient form of transport, and the Mortuary Temple, no long needed, became a depôt for a brewery firm.

If it has become difficult to understand fully the confidence that the carved angels and decorative flounces at Redfern and Rookwood actually offered comfort to the mourners who in customary suits of solemn black made their way up the steps and onto the platform to join the funeral train. We must remember that a funeral was a more important ceremony for Victorians than it is today – even poor families saved through a lifetime to provide for a 'respectable' funeral with at least one pall-bearer, though they could never hope to emulate the grandiose ceremonies of the rich.

 Regent Street, Redfern

Mortuary Temple

SYDNEY TOWN HALL

Prince Albert, Duke of Edinburgh, laid the foundation stone of Sydney Town Hall in April 1868, just a month before he was shot in the back by a renegade Irishman at a picnic at Clontarf. It seemed for a while as though the project might share in the bad luck, for its first architect, J. H. Wilson, a previously unknown Tasmanian who had won the competition for a design, suddenly died. A succession of architects muddled their way through to the completion of the first section of the building in 1869, then the addition of a mansard roof and vestibule (by Albert Bond) and the clock tower (Thomas and Edward Bradridge) before in 1889 the City Architect, Thomas Sapsford, presided over the completion of the Centennial Hall and the remainder of the building.

If the idea had been to compete with Melbourne's magnificent Town Hall, Sydney can have said to have succeeded – the Centennial Hall alone (known originally as the Palace of Democracy) is a triumph of engineering.

Sydney Town Hall was celebrated, on its completion, as the grandest civic centre in the British Empire. For now obscure reasons its site was by no means the most impressive available; it seems to have been squabbling between the British Government and the Town Council that resulted in the Hall being built some distance from Government House and the then CBD, on uncertain ground next to St Andrew's Cathedral – ground which had for decades been used as a cemetery, so that the first task was the exhumation of a large number of bodies. On its completion, however, the building was generally considered a triumph, with its grand porte-cochère (later demolished when the building of a railway tunnel threatened the building's stability) and a clock tower taller than any other in Australia apart from Sydney's own Post Office. Particularly admired was the use of Australian flora in its decoration, announced right at the entrance, where the city's coat of arms is surrounded by sandstone carvings of ferns, waratahs and cabbage palms, with lyrebirds and cockatoos.

Sydney Town Hall

Australian history was celebrated elsewhere in stained glass: the Captain Cook window shows Cook flanked by the Endeavour and the Discovery, with globe, chart, anchor, bunting and oars, and English flowers. The Australia window, designed (as they all were) by Lucien Henry, has New South Wales represented as Oceania, ruler of the southern seas, clothed in the Union Jack and the flag of St George, her headdress made of good Australian wool and decorated with ram's horns, holding a miner's lamp and a trident.

The Town Hall was gradually allowed to grow somewhat shabby, and was taken in hand in the 1990s by the heritage architect Howard Tanner, brilliantly repaired to be reopened by the Queen in 1992. Neglected features were repaired and in some cases restored – the faux marble pillars in the Centennial Hall were seen for the first time (included in the original plans they had never been put in place).

Perhaps the grandest feature of this great hall is its magnificent 1889 organ, built by Hill & Son of London, and still the largest in the world. The wonder of its splendidly decorative case is equalled by the immensity and sumptuousness of its tone; the sound of its 64-foot contra trombone stop was somewhat blasphemously compared to the probable sound of the last trump.

23 483 George Street, Sydney

THE NECROPOLIS

With the growth of the city, the cemeteries established in the early years of Sydney – first at Dawes Point, then near what is now Wynyard Station, and finally on the site of the Town Hall became seriously overcrowded, and in 1862 the government bought eighty hectares of land conveniently close to the railway line between the city and Parramatta. In 1868 the first burial – of a young pauper – took place at what became known as the Rookwood Necropolis.

Over a million burials are believed to have taken place here, in what is believed to be the largest cemetery in the southern hemisphere. The ground was originally divided into areas for the burial of people of different religious denominations, each area calculated according to the beliefs registered in the 1861 census. These were to be administered by separate boards of trustees, and are now managed by five denominational trusts.

The Necropolis is a testament to the racial and spiritual diversity of the city and the country; Muslims and Jews, Anglicans and Protestants, Greek Orthodox and Chinese sharing a carefully tended landscape.

The Necropolis is, like most cemeteries, a tranquil place. Row upon row of identical headstones, differing only in the names upon them and the languages in which the deceased are commemorated, contrast with the more elaborate tombs of the past – pinnacled miniature castles, handsome foursquare mansions, solid outsize stone caskets – which in their day must have been so expensive that only the very rich could have afforded them. Here and there a religious statue lifts a benignant hand or gestures skyward; crosses – plain and Celtic, Greek and Russian – preside over family graves. Headstones of black polished granite outface others of honey-coloured but already crumbling sandstone. However various the design or material of these, each is eventually ravaged by time, which has attacked the most elaborate tomb with the same inevitability as the poorest headstone. In older parts of the Necropolis row upon row of gravestones lean gently, the grass around them carefully cut, clearly unvisited for several lifetimes, the inscriptions on them now all but illegible. Some are smothered by overgrown rose-bushes, planted as a living memorial but now a mark of forgetfulness – just as, between two of them, a bare patch of earth marks the grave of a man or woman clearly forgotten almost as soon as he or she was laid to rest.

There are various memorial shrines, two of the most moving commemorating the victims of the Holocaust, and stillborn children and infants. The chapels of the various denominations also vary – from the almost clinical plainness of the Roman Catholic mausoleum to the delicacy of the Islamic monument, the prettiness of the Chinese temple and the Ukrainian priest vault, the no-nonsense statement of the Anglican Chapel and the handsome gesture of the Crown of Thorns Altar, dedicated to the dead of all denominations.

24 Centenary Drive, Rookwood

The Necropolis

THE FORTIFICATIONS

In the earliest years of the colony forts were built to defend Sydney Cove not only from invaders but from possible convict revolts. Forty years later, when British garrisons were withdrawn from Australia, the government built defences at Outer and Inner Middle Head, Georges Head, South Head, Steel Point and Bradley's Head – defences which because of developments in armaments were out of date almost before they were finished.

It was in the 1920s that more serious attention was paid to the defence of Port Jackson, with two 9.2-inch gun batteries of two guns each placed at North Head and Cape Banks, and supported by smaller guns elsewhere – a system which defended the coast from Broken Bay to the Royal National Park. These were well-designed and well-engineered defences, unlike those which were hastily thrown up at the start of World War II, during the panicky time when attack by Japanese ships seemed all too probable. This became a reality in May 1942, when the guns proved too badly sited to fire on the midget submarines which entered the harbour.

In 1804 Governor King suggested that a battery of twelve eighteen-pounder guns should be placed at South Head, but it was many years before such heavy artillery moved along Military Road to fortify the emplacements at Inner Head. In 1874 there were three 10-inch, two 9-inch and five 80-pounder guns in position, and four years later a torpedo firing station. In 1873 the novelist Anthony Trollope visited some of the fortifications and commented on the 'open batteries and casemated batteries, shell rooms and gunpowder magazines, barracks rising here and trenches dug there', all of them in such beautiful surroundings that, he thought, 'one would almost wish to be a gunner for the sake of being at one of these forts'.

The World War II fortifications were so carelessly erected and so ramshackle that time has disposed of them almost as completely as any enemy; there are few signs of the hundred anti-aircraft sites and searchlight positions of that period. Of the earlier fortifications, however, much is still to be seen.

North Fort provides examples, with the remains not only of the earlier works but of the underground command post and observation posts set up between 1935 and 1938. There are more elaborate examples at Middle Head, with underground tunnels, gunpowder magazine and underground power room supported by iron columns. Some of the tunnels were used to train troops destined for the Vietnam War to withstand interrogation under torture. On the surface, rather handsome Victorian Regency officers' quarters were built, designed by the Colonial Architect, and protected by a ditch-and-wall reminiscent of English moated houses. The Sydney Harbour Federation Trust is engaged in the preservation of the area and its military heritage.

The Fortifications

CARISBROOK HOUSE

Between the ramshackle houses of The Rocks, the terraces of the city and the villas of the upper middle class, the years between the 1860s and the 1880s saw the growth of comfortable small middle-class homes around the outskirts of the city. These might almost be described as cottages with ideas above their station, the 'front rooms' (drawing room and sitting room) on show to visitors, while a curtain in the hallway hid the back part of the house (the bedroom and kitchen) from inquisitive eyes.

An archetypal example is Carisbrook House, perched above Burns Bay, its garden running vertiginously down to the water's edge. It was built in the early 1880s by Rachel and Thomas Brooks, who originally lived down at the water's edge in a much smaller cottage. Local sandstone was probably quarried nearby, and the new house built higher up, perhaps to be convenient for the bridge, which was being planned to cross the river to Hunters Hill – previously reachable only by boat. The house was bought by Lane Cove Council in 1981, and a Government grant has enabled a handsome refurbishment.

The style and proportions of Carisbrook are typical of the sort of desirable house Australian architects were asked to provide in the 1880s – and just as with larger and more elaborate buildings, they looked to England and America for inspiration, turning the pages of such books as J. C. Loudon's English Encyclopaedia of Cottage, Farm and Villa Architecture or Calvert Vaux's American Villas and Cottages. These books illustrated small houses built sometimes of brick in a discreet Italianate style with traces of rustic gothic, commonly known as the *cottage orni*. They did not copy slavishly, however, building in sandstone when it was available, and adapting the designs to the climate of New South Wales, with (as here) French doors opening directly from the bedrooms onto open shaded balconies.

In time fashion dictated changes in taste, but happily Carisbrook survived almost entirely in its original state, by far the oldest house in its area, and under a Heritage Council conservation order since 1981. Like many other heritage houses it has become a museum, gradually and tactfully refurnished in the mid-Victorian style.

 334 Burns Bay Road, Lane Cove

EVELEIGH RAILWAY YARDS

The suburb of Eveleigh is about three kilometres south of Sydney's CBD, just east of the University of Sydney. Part of it is now confused with Redfern, which overtook it. Redfern Station was originally Eveleigh Station, and south-west of it was built, between 1880 and 1886, a large complex of railway workshops – over sixty acres of them – to service the engines and rolling stock of the growing NSW railway. In 1908 over three thousand workers were employed there, and a separate station – Macdonaldtown – was built in the middle of the yards to cope with the morning and evening rush hours.

By this time, the first steam locomotives to be built in Australia were being built at Eveleigh, and the workers were using some of the most modern technology available in the world. During both the first and second world wars part of the yards were occupied in making munitions. Construction of locomotives ceased in 1988, and the rail workshops were moved to Enfield in Sydney's inner west. In 1892 unions representing workers at Eveleigh were the first in Australia to negotiate a six-day working week; a quarter of a century later, when during the first world war a conservative Government attempted to introduce a new system of workers' control, those at Eveleigh downed tools in a strike which spread right across Australia. The Labour Movement has a deep nostalgic affection for the Eveleigh yards; happily, the area has not been allowed to become derelict.

The New South Wales government established the Australian Technology Park in 1991 and encouraged the use of part of the site as a theatre space. The Australian Technology Park is host to a diverse community of science, communications and IT companies, and provides excellent conferencing and exhibition venues. The Carriage Works – which included the two largest brick buildings in the southern hemisphere – have become a contemporary performing arts centre with, in Bay 17, a theatre which can seat eight hundred people and two more smaller theatre spaces. There are also two purpose-built rehearsal spaces, galleries, exhibition spaces, bars and restaurants.

Much of the area has been preserved to give a good general indication of its history: in bays one and two of the locomotive workshops building there is an industrial museum.

 Wilson Street, North Eveleigh

Eveleigh Railway Yards

CALLAN PARK

Callan Park Hospital for the Insane was built in 1885 on an estate originally bought almost fifty year earlier by a Crown Solicitor and police magistrate, John Ryan Brenan, who originally built Garry Owen House there. This was a fine house overlooking the Parramatta River, reached by a handsome tree-lined avenue entered from Balmain Road, through an elegant pair of wrought-iron gates.

Brenan entertained generously at Garry Owen House until bankruptcy forced him to sell. In 1873 the Colonial Government bought the estate with the intention of establishing a 'lunatic asylum' there based on the theories of the American Quaker Dr Thomas Kirkbride, who advised the kindly treatment of the mentally ill, with a pleasant environment and personal wellbeing as prerequisites.

The result was a set of sandstone buildings with spacious rooms fronted by generous verandahs; male and female quarters were linked, and the rooms varied in design and construction to accommodate patients with various degrees of mental illness, varying from 'noisy and violent' to 'quiet and convalescent'. Outside, the grounds were laid out by Charles Moore, the Director of the Botanic Gardens. Over a thousand patients overcrowded the complex in the 1890s and though the institution remained open until 1994, the decay of the idea of institutionalised treatment for the mentally ill meant that inmates were gradually placed in local communities. Eventually Sydney College of the Arts took over the main buildings, which today house painters, print-makers, potters and other artists.

Apart from its beauty – and Moore did his work well – Callan Park itself contains many historically interesting buildings, more or less well preserved and cared for. Brenan's original Garry Owen House eventually became a nurses' training school, and though much altered over the years it remains a handsome building in the Greek Revival style. It now houses the New South Wales Writers' Centre.

Unfortunately Broughton House – the only survivor of three fine villas built in the 1840s, which was a convalescent hospital during the first World War, then an army hospital, and finally a teaching hospital – has been neglected and vandalised, and its original grandeur (it had some twenty rooms) is now much decayed, as indeed are a number of smaller buildings in the Park, which have sometimes been vandalised and are sometimes simply gently decaying. There is an echo of London at the main entrance; the columns are reproductions of those at famous Newgate Gaol.

 Balmain Road, Lilyfield

Callan Park

FORT DENISON

Fort Denison, with its Martello tower, has proudly sailed the waters of Port Jackson for a century and a half.

When the First Fleet arrived in 1788, there was of course no building on the rough outcrop of rock north of the piece of land where Australia's first farm was established. The Eora tribe called it Mat-te-wam-ye; Governor Philip and his men called it simply Rock Island until it struck them that it was an ideal place to which to banish troublesome convicts. Only a couple of months after the first landing James Tenhel was found guilty of stealing tuppence-worth of bread from another convict. Because one of the officers described him to the Judge-Advocate as 'remarkably peaceful and obedient to command', rather than being flogged he was sentenced to 'a week's confinement on bread and water on a small rocky island near the entrance of the cove'. Henceforth the island was known, graphically, as Pinchgut.

Pinchgut was an excellent place of detention, sharks in the surrounding waters making the idea of escape unattractive. There was also fifteen metres of good sandstone above the waterline, and renegade convicts were set to work quarrying it for use in building what is now Circular Quay. Some years later the island's prominence made it an excellent site for a gibbet; the first man to be executed on Pinchgut seems to have been Francis Morgan, a murderer whose last words are said to have been an exclamation about the beauty of the last view he was to see. His body and those of subsequent hanged men were left to swing until they rotted.

Pinchgut's transformation into a more respectable place began in 1839, when a fort was planned as part of lively attention to the port's security. The careful removal of the available sandstone from the island meant that eight thousand tons of it now had to be fetched from Kurraba Point, Neutral Bay – but it was not until 1855 and a panic fear of invasion by the Russians during the Crimean War that work was completed, and Pinchgut was renamed Fort Denison after the then Governor of New South Wales, Sir William Denison.

The main feature of the fort is its Martello tower, the only one in the southern hemisphere. Highly resistant to attack, these towers proliferated around Europe during the nineteenth century, and it must have seemed an obvious pattern to follow at Port Jackson. A proud officer commanded twenty-four soldiers whose armament consisted of three 8-inch muzzle-loaders in the tower, with two ten-inch and twelve 32-pounders outside. There is also a tide gauge, still working.

Alas, the three cannon would have been no use at all in conflict: they could not cover enough of the harbour through the narrow embrasures, and the recoil would have destroyed the small room in which they were placed. But shortly after their installation Charles Lightoller, a lively young officer from a visiting P&O liner, sneaked out at night, hoisted a fake Boer flag at the fort, and set off one of the cannons, causing broken windows and panic in the town. Years later, Lightoller was the most senior officer to survive the Titanic disaster. A cannon is now fired, more innocently, at 1pm every day, a tradition which started in 1906 to enable visiting ships to set their chronometers.

28 Access is via ferries or excursion boats from Circular Quay

Building Sydney's History

THE STRAND ARCADE

The Strand Arcade, running between Pitt and George Streets, was the last of five grand shopping arcades which once distinguished Sydney's city centre. During the crass demolition and redevelopment of the 1960s, the splendid Imperial Arcade, the domed Victoria Arcade, the elegant Royal Arcade and the Piccadilly Arcade were all destroyed. Only the Strand remains.

It opened in 1892, designed by the British architect John Spencer and distinguished by elegance rather than opulence. Its fine cedar staircases – one at each end of its 193 metre stretch – lead up to two galleries, the top one of which overhangs the other to provide shade. The slim marble columns, the decorative balustrades and the Victorian tiled floors are all in evidence, as are the hydraulic lifts. But all is the result of meticulous rebuilding after a disastrous fire in 1977, which left only the Pitt Street façade intact. The arcade narrowly escaped complete demolition, Sydneysiders, now recognising the folly of previous destruction, mounted an insistent campaign for its rebuilding, and it now looks as it ever looked. Only missing are the two large chandeliers with fifty gas jets and fifty electric lamps in each; the original building had been the first in the city to use a combined gas and electric system.

The reconstruction of the Strand Arcade is a tribute not only to the public, who insisted on it, but to those who financed and carried out the work, restorers grubbing about in the fire-damaged ruins to find small pieces of wood and glass to give them evidence for duplicating the original as accurately as possible.

'The finest public thoroughfare in the Australian colonies', as it was called when it opened, had, as it still has, lines of elegant shops on all three levels – 80 shop-fronts in each case. The basement, however, has had a rather more chequered history. In the 1920s it housed The Ambassadors Café, which was in fact a nightclub rather than a restaurant. Its premises comprised the basement of the Strand, but also a large space excavated under neighbouring premises in Pitt Street. There were two ballrooms, a small Palm Court where one could lunch or enjoy an afternoon tea-dance, and eight private saloons which could be hired for private delights. It was said that seven hundred people could be entertained at the Ambassadors at one time, and that on one evening in 1927 the guests included the Duke and Duchess of York, then on their Australian tour. A less reputable night-club, the Chequers, took the place of the Ambassadors in the 1950s.

 412-414 George Street, Sydney

The Strand Arcade

THE QUEEN VICTORIA BUILDING

Described by one fashion commentator as 'the most beautiful shopping arcade in the world', the Queen Victoria Building sails along between George and York Streets, a stately galleon, impossible to ignore, determined to impress.

It was designed in 1892 in the Romanesque Revival style, then highly fashionable and popular in America. Incorporating an enthusiastic use of eleventh and twelfth century French, Spanish and Italian features, it offered the architect the opportunity to provide the QVB – as it is always called – with a riot of striking features including a large central dome (joined on the roof by other smaller domes), arched skylights, colonnades, arches, balustrades and cupolas. This exterior richness is joined, on the George Street façade, by six massive symbolic semi-nude figures, allegedly symbolising national unity, the arts, science, labour, justice and business. The interior is lit by stained-glass windows and exhibits a Royal Clock exhibiting tableaux from English life, and a Great Australian Clock with scenes from Australian history. These, in questionable taste, are modern additions, as are the obligatory escalators which, however, have been rendered more or less inoffensive by the ingenious use of reflective glass and mirrors.

The Queen Victoria Building

aThe QVB stands on the site of the original Sydney open-air market established in 1810 on a rectangle of land between George, Market, York and Druitt Streets. In 1883 it was decided to replace this with a market building which would also have space for shops – a sort of undercover shopping street – and the then city architect, George McRae, was asked to provide designs. At a time of flux in architectural design, he prepared not one but four sets of plans: one in the Gothic style, one Renaissance, one Queen Anne and one Romanesque. Though councillors found the Romanesque design 'rather startling' – so many domes! – it was accepted, and building work started at the end of 1893. Another ten years on, the 'magnificent pile of buildings', as the Lord Mayor called it, was opened.

There was some difficulty in finding tenants for the shops which ran along both sides of the three storeys above the basement where the market business was done. A great variety of businesses moved in, but only a proportion of the available shops were let during the first year. Though these had increased to almost the full number by 1914, that was the apogee of business, and a gradual decline in tenancies began to worry the Council. Moreover, changes in architectural fashion began to make the QVB seem old-fashioned, and a headline in 1927 declared WHITE ELEPHANT TO GO – the first hint of possible demolition.

The Council seemed to lose its nerve where the building was concerned. They failed to take advantage of the general boom in business in the 1930s to refurbish the QVB – instead moving the Electricity Department into the building, and wrecking much of the interior to install inappropriate art deco features. It seemed the beginning of the end, with almost every interior feature of the building brutalised. Part of the basement became a garage, and

Building Sydney's History

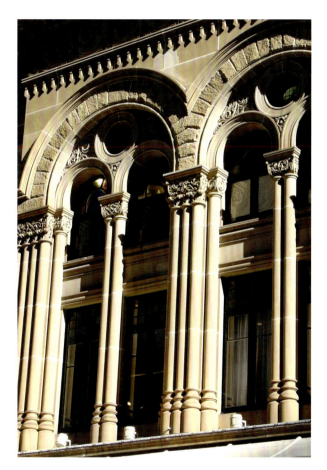

Fortunately the wrecking of other landmark buildings – notably almost all of the other smaller arcades – sounded a warning, and the QVB in the end – against the odds – survived. In 1959 the Council recognised the value of the building (by now some $30 million) and agreed to spend four million on restoration – only to back out when it seemed that considerably more money would be needed. In the end a partnership was established with a developer, Ipoh Garden, and in 1986 the building was reopened, meticulously restored, its economic viability bolstered by a huge underground car park beneath York Street.

The QVB is now a monumental tribute to those who at last recognised that the demolition of every building which suddenly seems antique or old-fashioned is a retrograde act.

30 455 George Street, Sydney

the City Rat-Catcher occupied one of the shops. During the Second World War concrete bomb shelters were built, and a hole was knocked in the central dome through which fire-spotters could watch for Japanese bombers. The inside of the building by now scarcely resembled what it had been: cheap partitioning created a series of rooms where there had been none, architectural details had been wrenched out . . .

BORONIA HOUSE

In 1855 Vincenz Zabul, who had arrived in Australia nineteen years earlier, bought for £10 a parcel of land at the top of a hill on the north shore, with splendid views over Sirius and Hunters Bays. For over thirty years it lay unused, but then the establishment of a regular ferry service and the promise of the coming of the tramways started the inevitable march of Mosman towards its eventual status as one of the most desirable suburbs of Sydney.

Zabul's land became highly sought-after, particularly by such men as the enterprising local entrepreneur Richard Haynes Harnett, who had already begun to build a number of grand houses designed by the Sydney architects Sheerin and Hennessy for the up-and-coming upper middle class of Sydney.

Twin villas Boronia and Telopea were not in fact built by Harnett, but by a bricklayer and a carpenter, John and Michael Kearey, using local sandstone from a nearby quarry for the plinths, and bricks bought from Harnett for the remainder of the buildings – so far the only two grand villas in Military Road. Boronia and Telopea were guarded by sandstone walls and a cast iron fence and gates. Camphor laurels stood beside the entrance to Boronia's carriage drive, which circled a large flower bed. There were equally generous gardens behind the house, with shrubberies, a magnolia tree, an orchard, a grass tennis court, a well, and stables.

Boronia's twin house, Telopea, next door to the west, has been thoroughly vandalised: the remains of the old house cower within an ugly modern façade, the decorative ironwork wrenched off, the gardens now a car-wash. A few beautiful old tiles remain.

Boronia is substantially what it was when the financial broker George William Godwin moved into it in 1896. The Godwins made a few more domestic alterations in the 1920s, including building a fern house outside the drawing-room, with fanlights of figured, brightly coloured glass.

The reason why all this can still be seen – why Boronia has survived when so many fine, sturdy villas of the period have been demolished to make way for more profitable buildings – is that in 1952 it was bought by Mosman Council for use as the borough's library. Happily by 1979, when the library moved out, the Heritage Council had placed a permanent preservation order on the house.

 624 Military Road, Mosman

CENTRAL STATION

The first railway in New South Wales connected Sydney and Parramatta, and was opened in 1855, with a somewhat basic terminus – one wooden platform and a corrugated iron shed – near the site of the present Central Station. A larger terminus opened in 1874 with, eventually, fourteen platforms. These were demolished one-by-one and replaced as the present building was erected in 1906, replacing a convent, a police station and a cemetery. As the Devonshire Street cemetery had been used for most Sydney burials between 1820 and 1860 the bodies had to be exhumed and re-buried in 1901 before the building of Central Station could begin.

The 1906 building has grown over the years, the most notable addition to the original plan being the clock tower, which appeared in 1921. The style of the building, with its large vaulted roof over the original fifteen platforms, referred to the almost cathedral-like dimensions of railway termini elsewhere, the growth of the railway systems offering architects unusual opportunities for work on a grand scale. The architect of 'the grandest railway station in Australia' was the Government Architect, W. L. Vernon.

Compared to some of the palatial railway termini of Europe, and even to Melbourne's Flinders Street station, the Sydney Central station is relatively restrained – the façade only enlivened by a double row of piers – sandstone, of course. As is the case at most major termini, Platform One is the platform which has been the most prominent: distinguished visitors have been ceremoniously greeted there throughout the years; the Governor's Archway led from the platform to the roadway where his coach or car awaited him. Nearby is Ambulance Avenue, where horse-drawn and later motorised ambulances could have a clear way past traffic in case of emergency. The second and third floors of the central building went up at the same time as the clock tower, with offices for the chief traffic manager.

Many changes and alterations have inevitably taken place in the interior of the station and resulted in the loss of original features – but at least some have been preserved: the original indicator boards are in the Powerhouse Museum, as is the row of clocks which originally announced the time of train departures. The original ticket office has survived in situ, with fine stained-glass windows, murals, and an inlaid map on the floor, with the crests of the state. Alas, it is now a fast-food outlet.

Devonshire Street, which crossed the original site, has survived as a tunnel which crosses under the station, and popularly retains its name. The first Sydney underground railway line, the city circle, opened in 1926 (though it did not include Circular Quay until 1956). The Central Station is above ground, but deep underground platforms 24 and 25 serve the Eastern Suburbs line. Do not however wait for trains on platforms 26 or 27; they have never been used.

 Eddy Avenue, Central

Central Station

THE FINGER WHARF, WOOLLOOMOOLOO

Now a fashionable centre for diners and wealthy residents, the Finger Wharf at Woolloomooloo was for over seventy years a working jetty, in the first instance for the export of wool. The Sydney Harbour Trust built the wharf between 1911 and 1915, and it was designed by the Trust's Dublin-born Chief Engineer, Henry Walsh, who also constructed wharves at Walsh Bay and Jones Bay. Still claimed as the largest timber-piled building in the world, the Finger Wharf stands four hundred metres long and sixty-three wide, supported above the waters of the bay by three thousand six hundred piles.

Originally a covered roadway struck up the centre of the wharf, with sheds on each side and loading and unloading going on to left and right. At the northern end was a large carpenters' shop. Some care was obviously taken for the look of the wharf, and its three gable roofs and gridded façades were always relatively handsome. When it fell into disuse the State Government cheerfully proposed its demolition. The public had other ideas, and protests saved what is now recognised as an iconic building.

Work at the Finger Wharf was hard and poorly paid. During the depression, the 'bull system' meant that casual labour was hired on the basis of brawn, and weaker and older men went to the wall. Apart from the wharf's commercial use, it saw the melancholy embarkation of troops during both world wars. The Anzacs sailed from here to Gallipoli, and prisoners returned from Changi. Between and after the wars emigrant ships also docked here – many of the 'ten pound Poms' landed at Woolloomooloo. Cruise liners also frequently docked, until the terminal at Circular Quay and others nearer the city centre took over that traffic. The State Government, calling it an 'eyesore', proposed and designed a marina resort complex to replace the wharf, and demolition was scheduled for January 1991. Local residents however stood and sat in the way of the workers – who in any case were sympathetic to a 'green ban' which was imposed by the trade unions.

After a year of controversy during which the State Government vowed to let the wharf 'lie there and rot', plans were revised and the original structure was saved. It now supports a boutique hotel at its south end, and a number of large and small private apartments ranging from single rooms to a luxury penthouse occupied by a famous film actor. Where the carpenter's shop once stood there is now a concrete and steel apartment building, separated from the main building.

The finger wharf became, and still is, one of the most fashionable and expensive places in the city in which to live. The conversion of the interior of the former packing sheds has been ingeniously done, still affording a certain amount of public access, while along the whole length of the east side of the wharf a series of fashionable restaurants draws crowds of diners.

The relationship between the wharf and the local area is still somewhat equivocal. Many of the wharfies lived locally, and some of the streets in which they lived are not greatly changed. The celebrated 'Café de Wheels' near the entrance to the wharf is a great deal closer to the original spirit of the wharf than the luxury restaurants. Woolloomooloo has not yet been 'gentrified', though the process is beginning.

 Cowper Wharf Roadway, Woolloomooloo.

The Finger Wharf, Woolloomooloo

BABWORTH HOUSE

Babworth House, at Darling Point, was built in 1912-15 by Samuel Hordern, the twice-knighted businessman whose store was a flagship of the Sydney retail trade. Designed by the architects Morrow and De Putron, it has been described as of national significance both historically and aesthetically, unique in its architectural detailing, its Art Nouveau and neoclassical motifs 'of a standard and form rarely seen in domestic architecture'.

In an area where impressive houses were becoming the norm, Hordern had his architects contrive an original building, with unpredictable gables and unexpected covered balconies with circular or bowed fronts. The slate roof has terracotta ridges, copper guttering and downpipes, all specially designed. Babworth contained over forty rooms, the interior, when the house was completed, presenting an anthology of Classical, Art Nouveau and Edwardian features. The ground floor hall, stair hall, dining and drawing rooms, ballroom/billiard room, library and smoking room were panelled in English oak and Queensland maple, with decorative detail which while somewhat ostentatious was always beautifully rendered. Upstairs, the main bedrooms and dressing rooms had equally extensive carved timber fittings.

Babworth, on the site of an earlier house, Mount Adelaide (built in 1833 by former convict William Macdonald) was the Horderns' family home for forty years. Sir Samuel had married the daughter of a shipping magnate, and their combined fortunes made economy unnecessary. Even after the First World War, they were able to maintain the large number of servants necessary to run a large establishment. No expense was spared in the design of the house or gardens, with grottoes and rockeries, paths, balustraded Italianate garden terrace and stairways. Some rare indigenous plants which grew on the land before Mount Adelaide was built still remain, together with others dating from the nineteenth century. That much of this has survived is almost miraculous. After Sir Samuel Hordern's death in 1956 the contents of the house were sold and after much discussion Babworth became first a convalescent hospital, then an after-care unit. In 1981 it was closed for some years before housing a hospice, then in 1989 a nurses' home. Finally, the house was split into five large apartments, great care taken to conserve the house (whose exterior had deteriorated over the years). The extent of the gardens has been reduced, ten new houses having been built during 2002-4.

34 Mount Adelaide Road, Darling Point

THE COMMONWEALTH BANK AND MARTIN PLACE

The Commonwealth Savings Bank building is one of the grandest of all the buildings in Martin Place, which over the years became the largest civic space in Sydney, displaying some of the city's most imposing buildings. Built in 1916, the Commonwealth Bank was carefully conserved at the end of the 1980s, and is one of the best examples in the city of the preservation of architectural heritage.

The massive Ionic columns and pilasters faced with glazed ceramic tiles are among the earliest examples in the city of a style which developed into Art Deco, while the use of red granite adds charm to the solidity of the building. That the façade is still intact is admirable; that the interior has been preserved is a splendid bonus. A riot of marble and scagliola through the grand hall and banking chamber enhances massive columns with neo-classical detail, and the lobby which connects Castlereagh and Elizabeth Streets, with its lift doors and noble staircase, boasts a giant barrel-vaulted stained-glass ceiling over the stairs.

If the Commonwealth Bank building remains the most impressive in Martin Place, others almost match it in grandeur. The General Post Office is certainly the largest, built between 1866 and 1891 amid huge controversy over its cost and design. It was seen from the start as a building which would symbolise the increasing power and wealth of the city. In 1966 it was sold and refurbished to hold shops and a hotel with a sensitively designed atrium and is now known as the GPO.

A block of land opposite the Post Office was sold by the city council in the 1890s, when its expenditure on the QVB (see p.150) had almost bankrupted it. On the site was built a number of buildings including the Art Deco Challis House and the offices of the Colonial Mutual Life Assurance Society, whose 1970s twenty-storey glass-walled tower has been much admired. The appearance of the Commonwealth Bank of Australia

head office on the corner of Martin Place and Pitt Street was in the past familiar to almost all Australian children in the form of a moneybox given to every child who opened an account.

The former Bank of Australasia at no.2 Martin Place is a handsome Romanesque building which ceased to be a bank some years ago and is now available to retail outlets. Its interior is decorated with bronze, cedar, wrought iron and gold leaf. There are of course also modern buildings, including the MLC Centre, designed by Harry Seidler and built on the site of a number of handsome historic buildings. When it was built in 1977 it was the tallest reinforced concrete office building in Australia, and the tallest in the world outside America; it was also an example of the rampant redevelopment which destroyed so much of historic Sydney.

At the east end of Martin Place was originally a range of buildings whose destruction in a fire in 1890 opened it out to Macquarie Street. It would similarly have been driven east as far as York Street had not the banks in George Street (notably Westpac Bank at no. 341, with its magnificent 1927 banking hall and art deco boardroom) refused to give way.

Martin Place also contains the Cenotaph, designed by Australia's best-known sculptor, Sir Bernard Mackennal. His statues of servicemen were the subject of fierce criticism – as was the whole design. The 17-ton granite base was cut at Moruya quarry and dragged to the site from a barge at Circular Quay by a team of twenty horses. Martin Place itself opened as a plaza in 1891 and became traffic-free in 1971.

 Martin Place, Sydney

The Commonwealth Bank and Martin Place

SYDNEY FERRY WHARVES

As the population of Sydney began to spread along the shores of the harbour, a ferry service became inevitable, as did the placing of the ferry wharves – the central ones at Circular Quay, then others at Manly, Balmain, Watson's Bay, Mosman, Neutral Bay and elsewhere.

The wharves were at first rough and ready – sometimes merely a set of steps and a simple wooden platform, with perhaps a shelter of some kind against the weather. Then, as the various ferry companies began to prosper – the Australian Steam Conveyance Company, the Port Jackson Steam Boat Company, the Balmain New Ferry Company and the rest – the wharves gradually became more elaborate until in the 1920s, when Sydney Ferries gained a virtual monopoly, they took on a recognisably uniform look. One of the old curved shelters still remains at Balmain East. That wharf has retained some personality, and at Mosman there is a whiff of the past; but on the whole the attraction of the wharves of today is much more a matter of their position than of their design, which is mostly standardized and dull.

In the earliest days, the ferries and wharves mainly served those who travelled for pleasure. There was a busy 'picnic trade' at weekends, when there were regular services to sometimes doubtfully respectable pleasure gardens – Athol Gardens at Mosman, the Avenue Pleasure Grounds at Hunters Hill or Fairyland at Lane Cove. The 'seaside resort' of Manly had its own regular service from 1854, and the Manly Steamship Company not only built wharves but saltwater baths and tearooms to help boost trade. The Parramatta River had been a highway to business and pleasure ever since the earliest days of the colony, and by 1883 small steamboats jostled with larger steamers (which could not dock in shallow water; a private tramway ran passengers into the town). Another money-spinner for Sydney Ferries was its monopoly of the service to Taronga Zoo – only twopence for adults and a penny for children, return.

In 1904 refreshment rooms were built on the wharf at Watsons Bay; many others followed, and today serve coffee and snacks both to commuters and to the millions of tourists to whom even the relatively uniform wharves are considerably more attractive than the best-designed bus stops.

Circular Quay

NUTCOTE

Nutcote is a modest cottage designed by an eminent architect who was also responsible for a number of grand houses in Sydney. B. J. Waterhouse very probably accepted the commission because it came from May Gibbs, whose children's book Snugglepot and Cuddlepie had already become a classic by the time the house was built in 1925.

She asked for a house which had 'compactness, convenience and charm', and was also presumably within a modest budget, for the upper storey the architect suggested was never built. Whether by her request or Waterhouse's original notion, the building is in a Mediterranean style, with textured stucco walls, a roof of Spanish pan tiles, and a pair of Tuscan columns to the porch and verandah, with its wrought iron railing, overlooking Neutral Bay.

May Gibbs left her cottage to UNICEF, which, unable to own property, auctioned it. Its position made it ideal for demolition and redevelopment, but relatives and fans of her work formed a foundation and succeeded in getting the house protected by a conservation order. Now the property of North Sydney Council, it is a museum devoted to May Gibbs and her work.

Waterhouse was brought to Australia from England at the age of six, and in his early thirties formed a lasting partnership with J. W. H. Lake. After an emphasis on arts and crafts houses, a visit to Italy turned his enthusiasm and attention to a Mediterranean style, first seen at Nutcote, by far the smallest house he ever designed.

May Gibbs' garden, her passion, remains much as she planted it. The architect clearly took great care to fulfil his client's wishes about the interior of her cottage, with exposed beams in the living room (which runs the width of the house), built-in furniture designed by the architect, and a studio in which she could work, with large windows giving not only light, but a fine view over the bay. He contrived an interior design which suggests to the eye that the house is much more spacious than is actually the fact. The dining room is perfectly adequate and with an equally good view; the adjoining kitchen however is minuscule, and certainly supports the theory that the architect kept in mind May Gibbs' assertion that while she kept no servants she herself was totally uninterested in either housework or cooking.

 5 Wallaringa Avenue, Neutral Bay

THE DYMOCKS BUILDING

The Dymocks Building, generally known as the Block, was built in 1927-8 on the site of the Royal Hotel, where the booksellers had been renting space since 1890. They bought the hotel and the building next door, and erected a shopping arcade whose style owed much to developments in shopping arcade architecture in America.

The style chosen by architect F. H. B. Wilton (dismissed for drunkenness during construction) was 'Commercial Pallazo', which had been used for over a century for prominent buildings in London and New York, including banks and gentlemen's clubs. There were earlier examples, already, in Sydney – among them the Daily Telegraph building on the corner of King and Castlereagh Streets, the Perpetual Trustee Company building in Hunter Street and the Commonwealth Bank building opposite the General Post Office in Martin Place. However, the Dymocks building has its own character, with exterior classical pilasters, a pair of small balconies and a corbelled cornice, and terrazzo and marble floors, decorated ceilings and beautiful shop fronts in the interior. Necessary refurbishment has destroyed some interior details, but much of the original décor remains.

Discussing the Dymocks Building a year after it was finished, the journal *Building* spoke of the way in which shopping habits had changed since the appearance of the motor car. Shoppers now enjoyed large department stores and the Dymocks building offered 'the same preference to the small shopkeeper', for above the handsome entrance lobby with its terracotta cladding, mouldings and metal grilles, were corridors decorated in the same style, along which ranged rows of shops. 'The inclemency of the weather', as *Building* so rightly observed, 'will not affect the shoppers in these well lighted arcades'. Much of the block has survived unaltered, though there have been some adjustments in the interest of fire evacuation.

An aspect of building history in the city survives in the use on the façade of the block of 'architectural terracotta' made from burnt clay and provided by the Wunderlich Company, which recognising the probability of war in Europe set up business in Sydney and Melbourne, purchased clay-bearing land, and by 1916, when imported terracotta was no longer available, were supplying their own tiles, individually prepared and numbered for use in specific buildings.

 428 George Street, Sydney

The Dymocks Building

THE CAPITOL AND STATE THEATRES

In 1891-3 the Belmore Markets were built on a site between Campbell Street and Hay Street in the Haymarket, near what is now Central Station. The market was a failure, and in 1913 a circus, the Hippodrome, was built on part of the site. This too failed, and elaborate plans were prepared for the building of a theatre which would provide both live performances and films. The result was the Capitol, an 'atmospheric theatre', which opened in 1928 designed on American lines, its aim to convince the patrons that they were sitting under a brilliantly starry night sky.

The State Theatre in Market Street opened in 1929 specifically as a cinema – a 'palace of dreams' seating two thousand people – its interior a wild Gothic, Italian and Art Deco extravaganza of statues, plaster cast figures, elaborate detail and original paintings, some by distinguished Australian artists, including William Dobell and Charles Wheeler. The so-called Koh-i-Nor crystal chandelier which hangs over the auditorium weighs over four tonnes and is claimed to be the second largest in the world.

The Australian architect Henry Eli White was the builder of the State, the Capitol, the St James in Elizabeth Street (demolished in 1971 to make way for an office block) and the Majestic at Newtown (burned down in 1980, in somewhat suspicious circumstances). He owed much to the American John Eberson, who built over a hundred 'atmospheric theatres', specialising in settings in Italian Renaissance, Moorish Revival and Art Deco styles, which visualised the auditoria as a huge stage set representing an open-air setting. White toured America to study these theatres, and the result is still to be seen in the Capitol and State.

The Capitol has had a somewhat chequered history. The theatre rose within the walls of the old circus building, and its interior was much admired when 2,999 patrons attended its opening, walking through a replica of the courtyard of the Pitti Palace in Florence to sit in the stalls under a dark blue sky which, as the lights dimmed, sparkled brilliantly with stars. The Capitol theatre organ and orchestra entertained them, together with Ted Henkel and his band, a news film, and a Paramount featurette: Toddlers. During the Depression the theatre closed, and by the 1930s was known only for horror and western films; the famous Wurlitzer organ ceased to play in 1947, and parts of the building began to disintegrate. Throughout the 1970s sexploitation films just paid the theatre's way. But though the Capitol was continually threatened with demolition, the tide gradually turned. Classified by the National Trust in 1977 it has been splendidly restored and is now a thriving home for musicals. With rebuilding backstage it could become Sydney's much-needed full-scale opera house.

In contrast, the State has had a virtually untroubled life. 'The Empire's greatest theatre', as it was described, opened with the new 1929 movie The Patriot, with the 'debonair genius' Price Dunavy at 'the mighty Wurlitzer', the console in itself a work of art in white and gold, matching the gilded gates which are a feature of the proscenium walls. Among other facilities, a ballroom with a sprung wooden dance-floor was installed in the 1930s and is still in excellent condition, as is the theatre itself. The National Trust describes the State as 'a building of great historical significance and high architectural quality, the preservation of which is regarded as essential to our heritage'.

38 The Capitol Theatre, 13 Campbell Street, Haymarket

38 The State Theatre, 49 Market Street, Sydney

THE BATHERS' PAVILION

In 1907 there was a problem at Balmoral. 'A mother of girls' complained to the Sydney Morning Herald that young men had been bathing 'naked, but for a nondescript rag around their middle'. She advocated flogging as just punishment.

The law insisted that bathing suits must 'cover the body from the neck to the knee', and men who turned down the tops of their bathing costumes were prosecuted; there were even, later, fines for those who used their cars as changing booths. So the local Council put up a rough shed with changing rooms for men and women, and in 1929 the handsome Bathers' Pavilion was opened by the Mayor. Designed by the Council architect, it cost over £12,000, and had ample space for male and female bathers to change into their costumes with a minimum of display and a maximum of modesty. The difficulty of climbing into the cumbersome bathing costumes in public without being arrested meant that the Pavilion's changing rooms were a money-spinner until the 1950s, when the onward march of the bikini and disregard for Victorian regulations ended their usefulness.

The Pavilion went up in the middle of the Great Depression, only a few years before Mosman Council organised the construction of the elegant Esplanade, Promenade and Rotunda at Balmoral as part of their plans to provide employment; in the same year similar pavilions were opened at Bondi and Brighton Le Sands.

Alfred H. Hale, who designed the Pavilion, was an admirer of Frank Lloyd Wright and the other American architects who favoured the so-called 'Spanish Mission' style, much used in California for private houses and small commercial buildings. The long, low, white building has a concealed roof, and the only feature to rise above it is the low central tower roofed with orange terracotta tiles. What might otherwise be rather severe lines on the seaward façade of the building are relieved by its division into two ranges of four bays each, and by the arched, grilled openings of the bays. Its elegance is undeniable, and happily preserved.

By 1969, with even less public concern for modesty, a restaurant took the place of the ground floor changing rooms. Protected by a Permanent Conservation Order, the Bathers' Pavilion remains a highly successful restaurant – or rather, two: a gourmet restaurant and a café.

 4 The Esplanade, Balmoral

The Bathers' Pavilion

SYDNEY HARBOUR BRIDGE

The icon which made Sydney truly famous world-wide, the Sydney Harbour Bridge, was opened in 1932. But the idea had been around for some time. The convict architect Francis Greenway proposed a bridge as early as 1815, and discussion continued, prompted by the inconvenience of travelling 25 kilometres and crossing five bridges to get from the north shore to the city.

The problem was the form a bridge should take, and it was not until after the First World War that tenders were firmly requested for the building either of a cantilever or arch bridge to connect Dawes Point to Milsons Point. In 1924 the tender of Dorman Long and Co. of Middlesborough in England was accepted, work began, and eight years later the bridge was open to traffic.

The fact that the bridge is fifty metres wide and now carries eight traffic lanes and two railway lines (originally there were two tram tracks) is a tribute to the planners who foresaw the growth of traffic at a time when the bridge sometimes carried only one or two cars at a time.

A competition held in 1900 to find a design for a harbour bridge produced no winner, but twelve years later the civil engineer John J. C. Bradfield, who had worked on the Cataract and Burrinjuck dams, travelled through Europe and America studying the construction of various bridges, and produced a design based on the Hell Gate Bridge in New York City. This was accepted, and the detailed design was carried out by Sir Ralph Freeman, consulting engineer to Dorman Long and Co.

The statistics of Sydney Harbour Bridge are still impressive: 53,000 tonnes of steel trusses, six million hand-driven steel rivets, a span of 503 metres, a height of 134 metres, a total weight of 38,600 tonnes, 27,200 litres of paint. Though the expense – the total cost was £6.25 million – was criticised by rural Australians, the project gave employment to fourteen hundred men during the years of the great depression.

Eight hundred houses were swept away to accommodate the approach roads. Tunnels 36 metres long were dug in which the anchoring bearings of the bridge were secured; the foundations are twelve metres deep. Eighty percent of the steel was brought from England, the concrete produced in Australia.

The arch was constructed simultaneously from north and south shores, meeting at 4.15 p.m. on 19 August 1930 – a number of bets had been taken on whether the two halves would meet exactly; they did. Ferry passengers far below cheered, and the workmen were given two shillings each to drink the bridge's health. Seven of their mates died while working on the bridge – in contrast, 139 died during the building of the Brooklyn Bridge.

The bridge hangs 51 metres above the water of the harbour, the highest point of the arch standing 135 metres – but on hot days it can rise by 180mm, due to expansion of the metal (thus necessitating hinges at its base). Attention was paid to aesthetics – the four grey granite pylons designed by the Scottish architect Thomas Tait are completely unnecessary except for the look of the thing. In general the whole construction was much admired, though it almost immediately attracted the affectionate name of 'the coat-hanger'.

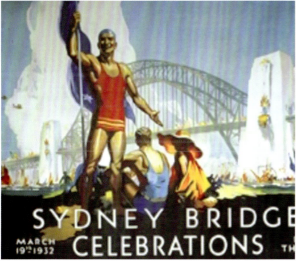

The bridge was severely tested on its completion: 96 steam locomotives, railway carriages, trams and lorries were packed to capacity onto the Bradford Highway – the official name of the road across the bridge – to ensure its safety. The Premier of New South Wales, Jack Lang, opened the bridge on 19 March 1932 – though unofficially pre-empted by Francis de Groot, a member of a right-wing political party, who rode his horse onto the bridge and slashed the ceremonial ribbon with his sword.

Today it is calculated that about 170,000 vehicles use the bridge every day; and with the opening of the harbour tunnel in 1992 the traffic has remained more or less under control. Maintenance costs amount to about $5 million a year, justifying the continuance of a toll originally raised to pay for the construction (cars at first charged sixpence each, a horse and rider threepence). Recently it has been possible to climb to the highest point of the bridge, a popular tourist attraction which has welcomed both children and centenarians. Easier is the climb to the top of the pylon lookout, reached via stairs in Cumberland Street, by walking from the lift in Circular Quay, or from Milsons Point station on the north shore. The pylon, apart from providing a fine view of Sydney and the harbour from 90 metres above the harbour, has a display on the history of the bridge.

 Bradfield Highway, Sydney

Sydney Harbour Bridge

THE STATE LIBRARY

Governor Lachlan Macquarie, speaking in 1813, hoped to see a library set up in Sydney but it was to be well over a century before the still unfinished State Library building was opened in 1943.

The founder of the library was to all intents the great Australian bibliophile David Scott Mitchell, the donation of whose collection to the state virtually forced the government to erect a building worthy to hold it. An ambitious design for the library came from the office of the Government Architect, and the construction of the Mitchell Wing was completed in 1908 – the year after Mitchell's death – with three reading rooms. It was much praised, but there were many delays before the rest of the building was even started, and acrimonious discussion about the various designs that were produced. In the end the principal librarian, William Herbert Ifould, was probably more responsible than anyone else for the final form taken by the building – described in one periodical as 'a real posh library', though it started life with a partial wartime blackout, the reading room unusable after dark.

In 1821 some private citizens started a subscription library (women were not eligible as members), but in 1838 the Government granted £4000 for the building of a Public Library and Museum, though it was not until 1869 that a free public library at last opened in a building on the corner of Bent and Macquarie streets. Over the next thirty years the library thrived, but the building became unsafe and inadequate. By 1889 it had so many books that some of its rooms had to be closed to make way for shelves on which to stack them.

As a result of pressure from Mitchell, the present site of the State Library was set aside in 1904 – against much opposition from some who believed that the building would obstruct entrance to the Domain, and others who asserted that people of 'an undesirable class' often frequented the area and would make visiting the Library uncomfortable. The Government Architect, Gorrie McLeish Blair, produced plans for a building criticised as being of 'vulgar ostentation', but it was nevertheless decided to start immediately on building one wing (Sydney was noted for its unfinished public buildings).

The pessimism of those who predicted that the library would remain for many years a work in progress was justified; it was not until 1942 that the complete building was opened to the public (even then with some areas yet to be finally completed). But in many respects it was and is extremely handsome, especially in some of its furnishings – the great bronze doors, for instance (which at the time provoked much controversy for their depiction of Aborigines), and the marble mosaic Tasman Map on the floor of the vestibule. The various stained glass windows were presented by benefactors, including two Sydney newspapers, who funded windows showing the publication of the first Sydney newspaper and Caxton with the first book printed in England. The Shakespeare Room, mooted as a celebration of the tercentenary of the poet's death, is a remarkable example of imitation Tudor design.

From the beginning the spacious reference reading room was greeted with enthusiasm, though in time a new annexe was inevitable, and was completed in 1988 – a tactful building which has seven floors below street level in order that its height matches that of the surrounding heritage buildings. It is connected by underground passage to the original building, and by a bridge to the first floor section now used as an exhibition space.

 Macquarie Street, Sydney

The State Library

WARRAGAMBA DAM

As long ago as 1845 it seemed to some people that the damming of the Warragamba River, a tributary of the Nepean, would be a clear and obvious answer to the problem of supplying growing Sydney with an adequate water supply. During severe droughts in the 1860s Lieut. Thomas Moore put the idea to a Commission of Enquiry but 'Nonsense!', came the reply; the notion was economically and technically impossible. This view continued to be held through a series of increasingly disastrous droughts in the 1890s and 1900s until at one period in the 1930s Sydney found itself with only enough water to last the population for six weeks.

This woke the Commissioners up, a weir was hastily built on the Warragamba, and at last plans were made for the building of a dam to close off a narrow gorge and form a lake which would become one of the largest reservoirs in the world. Three hundred thousand tonnes of concrete and two and a half million tonnes of sand and gravel later, the dam was complete, and now confines Lake Burragorang, which covers over nine thousand square kilometres and holds enough water to fill Sydney harbour four times.

Work began on the dam in 1948, and over two million tonnes of rock were excavated during the following five years. Then six hundred buckets riding an aerial rope-way brought sand and gravel from the Nepean River, and concrete was poured every day between June 1953 and the completion of the project in 1960. The first prestressed concrete tower in Australia was built to house ice-making equipment: ice was mixed with the concrete to prevent overheating as it set. Floods continually hampered and delayed the work (fourteen separate inundations in 1956 alone); enormous quantities of debris and silt were removed after each incident. The dam was raised by 5 metres in 1989, and work in 2006 increased the reservoir's capacity.

In such a project more statistics cannot be avoided: the dam rises 142 metres from its 104-metre-thick base, tapering to 8.5 metres at the top. Lake Burragorang holds 2,031,000 million litres of water when full, has a surface area of 75 square kilometres, is 52 kilometres long and anyone deciding to walk around it must trudge 354 km.

CHIFLEY SQUARE

Chifley Square is a truncated version of a public space originally planned to occupy most of the area between Philip and Macquarie, Loftus and Hunter Streets. It is now a sort of crooked triangle – the result of much argument and discussion between the two world wars. In the 1920s the spot was proposed as a natural extension of Elizabeth Street, but by 1937 there was general agreement to block off the end of Phillip Street to make a pedestrian precinct. A year later opinion had swung behind the idea of a formal square on an eighteenth-century model

None of these plans were carried through, and in 1957 the Qantas Building, with its graceful curved façade, virtually forced the shape of the present 'square' upon the planners. The unfortunate New Commonwealth Centre (1962) uglified the area until its happy demolition in the 1980s, by which time the Qantas Building had rescued it from insignificance. Now, the 'square', with the Chifley Plaza mirroring in distinction the Qantas building, is a bright and cheerful place in which to relax.

Both attractive and architecturally significant the Qantas building, in its time highly original as an office block, remains unique in Sydney. More perhaps by accident than design, the surrounding buildings have not only failed to diminish it, but sit comfortably around it, framing a highly attractive space, presided over by a witty sculpture portrait of a Labour Prime Minister, the eponymous Ben Chifley. The café which serves the granite courtyard is protected from the noise and grit of Hunter Street by a so-called 'Lightwall' – a long east-west glass fence, opaque at one end, translucent at the other. Benches sit beneath a network of palms.

As far as height goes, the post-modern art-deco Chifley Tower – said to have cost over a billion dollars to build – dominates the area, set between Hunter, Phillip and Bent Streets. The site alone cost three hundred and six million dollars in 1993, and the interest on the sum was over a million dollars a week, so construction was spectacularly swift – building took place simultaneously with the demolition of a twenty-storey building on the same site.

At the time of writing the building is still claimed, when measured to the top of its spire, to be the tallest building in Sydney. It boasts a massive steel pendulum weighing four hundred tonnes, held at rooftop level and connected to a hydraulic dampened gravity system which stops the tower swaying in high winds. There is a handsomely designed two level retail area giving onto the square. The side of the tower which faces the harbour consists of a vast glass sail, said to symbolise the spirit of the city. An historical footnote is that it was, until his bankruptcy, named after the financier Alan Bond.

Chifley Square, Sydney

Chifley Square

THE OPERA HOUSE

The Opera House is not only one of Sydney's or Australia's iconic buildings, but a masterpiece of world architecture listed as a UNESCO World Heritage Site. Designed and built between 1955 and 1973, its architect was the Dane Jørn Utzon.

With its million and more white and cream coloured Swedish tiles and pink Tarana granite, the exterior of the Opera House would be spectacular even without the extraordinary sweep of its seemingly wall-less segmented shape and rippling waves of steps. It appears to owe nothing to any building built before it, and it has had little influence on subsequent designs. It seems almost like some huge artefact suddenly revealed from another time and another space.

Over seven million people visit it every year – not only to attend concerts, plays, and performances of opera and ballet, but simply to be able to say that they have stepped inside a world famous building. They emerge impressed by the interior with its great sweeping arcs of concrete, one moment reminding one of being inside a giant upturned boat, the next resembling a huge set of organ pipes.

The drama of the Opera House's history matches the drama of its appearance. In 1954 the conductor Sir Leon Goossens persuaded the then Premier of New South Wales, Joseph Cahill, to instigate a design competition for an opera house on the site of a disused tram depot at Bennelong Point, named for the best-known of the Aboriginals befriended by members of the First Fleet.

The competition's prize of $5000 was won by the Danish architect Jørn Utzon. Though his design was universally admired, turning it into a set of practical building instructions was more difficult and there were continual delays and mounting costs. It was not until 1963 that practical problems seemed to be solved, and Utzon set up his office in Sydney to oversee the construction. In 1965 the mildly enthusiastic Labour premier Cahill was replaced by Robert Askin, a Liberal who had fought against the project since its inception. Costs seemed at that time more or less under control, at $22.9 million (eventually this mounted to a final $102 million), but Askin appointed a philistine Minister for Public Works, Davis Hughes, who was positively obstructive, and by February of 1966 Utzon was owed over $100,000 in fees. When Hughes withheld funding so that the architect could not even pay his staff, Utzon could see no alternative to resignation. He left Sydney, and never returned.

Architects, artists, actors and film-makers organised protests and marches, but terrified by escalating costs the politicians began to pare back and alter the scheme. A new team of architects radically altered Utzon's design: the larger of the two halls, which was to have been an opera house, became merely a concert hall with indifferent acoustics, while the smaller hall became an inadequate opera house, too small for major opera productions and with a dangerously undersized orchestra pit which threatens the hearing of the musicians. The seating accommodation in the concert hall was raised from 2000 to 3000, with more or less disastrous changes to the shape of the stage, the placing of lifts, and the whole backstage arrangements including dressing-rooms. The stage machinery installed in the large hall was dismantled and thrown out. A cinema, library and theatre were first added, then removed – finally they became two theatres and a studio space. Utzon's plans for the interior decoration, which

included impressive corridors lined with plywood, were scrapped. The designs of his acoustic consultant were ignored, with resultant problems.

The Opera House was opened by the Queen in 1973. Jørn Utzon was not invited to the ceremony, during which his name was not mentioned.

In the 1990s there began some plans to re-evaluate Utzon's original designs, and the architect was contacted by the Opera House Trust, which appointed him as design consultant for new work; the first space to be re-designed to his suggestion was named the Utzon Room. When he died in 2008 there was a state memorial service attended by his son, and by 2009 the western foyers had been spectacularly redesigned, with some hints of the elegance of Utzon's original vision. Before he died he put forward plans for a major reconstruction of the Opera Theatre. The rebirth of the whole complex to Utzon's original vision would be magnificent reparation for the farce which attended the building of the House. A recent grant has been put to the building of a tunnel for the transport of scenery; major expenditure will be needed to correct basic inadequacies which in 2010 led to work and safety issues, backstage.

 Bennelong Point

Opera House

BLUES POINT TOWER

Arriving at Sydney by sea, having sailed through the waters of Port Jackson agreeing wholly with the opinion of the first Europeans to see it that this is certainly the most beautiful harbour in the world, one finally comes in sight of those two icons, the Opera House and the Harbour Bridge. And right at the centre of the prospect of the Bridge is an uncompromising vertical high-rise building which immediately provokes the question, 'Who in their right mind allowed that to be built there?'

It is not simply that Blues Point Tower is a peculiarly ugly building, though that is the general opinion; it is simply that placed where it is it has the impact of an unnecessary exclamation mark in the middle of a well-crafted piece of prose. It draws the eye to it as any obtrusive object will do when completely inappropriate to its setting. So out of place to be almost laughable, it has the effect, as one distressed visitor observed, of making it seem that the bridge has grown a third leg.

Blues Point Tower, designed by the late Harry Seidler, was built at McMahons Point in 1962, and until 1970 was Australia's tallest building. The original idea had been for two shorter buildings, but the architect eventually decided to place one on top of the other in one 83-metre – tall block with twenty-four floors. His ambition was to make this the centre of a group of seven or eight similar towers. The plan happily came to nothing. To those who claimed that the Tower was Australia's ugliest building, Seidler replied that this was an opinion put about by the press, and that anyone who couldn't appreciate his building should go back to school

Setting controversy aside, the historical importance of the building is that it was the first high-rise strata title apartment building in the world. The developer, Dick Dusseldorp, introduced 'strata title' to Australia as a form of ownership of apartments in multi-storey buildings which enabled them to be bought separately. This, while not necessarily excusing the presence of the Tower, has at least had beneficial results for many thousands of Australian home-owners.

44 1 Blues Point Road, McMahons Point

WARRINGAH MALL

Warringah Mall was the first open-air shopping mall in the Sydney area. Originally known as Piper's Foley, it opened in Brookville in 1963, with fifty-three stores. Roselands Shopping Centre opened in 1965, with the shops under cover; at first Warringah shops were open to the elements.

Warringah Mall developed slowly – it was ten years before the Myer store opened, together with fifty additional shops, and another ten before a cinema complex opened. It was in 1999 that the complex was re-opened after considerable development brought in a large food court and another sixty specialist stores. Eventually the mall hosted over three hundred stores besides such large enterprises as Big W, David Jones, Coles and Target. Though at the time of writing Westfield at Parramatta and Bondi Junction have greater floor-space, Warringah Mall is still the third largest shopping centre in New South Wales. Its architecture is functional and unexceptional, though care has been taken to preserve some trees, and the covered areas remain linked to some spaces open to the sky.

It was towards the end of the 1950s that shoppers began to look outside the large family-owned department stores of the city centre, and demand a similar service nearer their homes in the suburbs. Considerable thought was given to the design of these early experiments in mass suburban shopping areas. Top Ryde, as it was called, and Warringah Mall were distinctly different in character. Top Ryde, which opened in 1957, was entirely covered, offering the first pedestrian mall 'on American principles' which at the same time promised shoppers 'the carnival atmosphere of the old European marketplace.' There was a large department store surrounded by forty-four shops and served by a car park with seven hundred spaces and an excellent bus service. While Ryde offered shoppers pleasant balconies and indoor spaces in which to relax, Warringah had the advantages and disadvantages of being open to sun and rain – and indeed today

still has a central open area with a pleasant fountain and carefully preserved trees. Roselands, now a medium-sized shopping area, claimed when it opened to be the largest shopping centre in the southern hemisphere.

The inexorable march of the malls has resulted in a high degree of convenience to shoppers, but boarded shop windows in many suburban streets.

45 Corner of Condamine Street and Old Pittwater Road, Brookvale

Warringah Mall

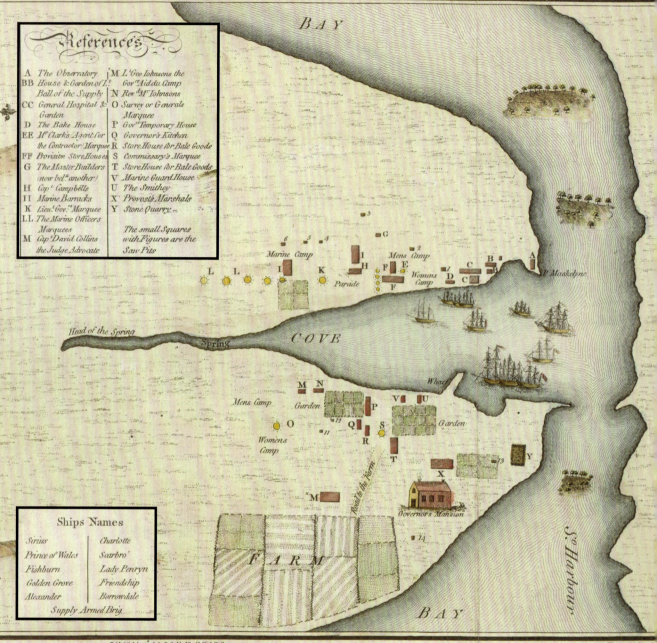

MAPPING SYDNEY'S HISTORY

This inaccurate but moving map of 'Sydney Cove' was drawn during the first months of the colony by convict Francis Fowkes, transported for stealing a greatcoat and a pair of boots. It gives a vivid impression of the little settlement, uneasily perched astride the Tank Stream on the coast of a huge continent. The 'Governor's Mansion' (bottom, right) was in reality yet to be built – he used a prefabricated hut (marked P); but stone for more substantial buildings was already being quarried on the present site of the Opera House (marked Y). Across the harbour the precursor of the Observatory was already set up (A), near the camps for male and female convicts. Only one road is shown: 'the road to the farm' – a farm which looks large and prosperous, but which was already demonstrating how difficult it was to grow anything in the arid soil of Sydney. Watkin Tench, the marine officer who wrote by far the best account of the early years of the colony, recorded how quickly 'little edifices' were built by the convicts, and Governor Arthur Phillip was determination that the city which would grow on this spot should be a grand one, suitably matched in scale to the size of the country of which it would be the capital, with the principal streets two hundred feet wide and regulations preventing houses being huddled together, so that the city would be open to whatever breezes could alleviate the heat of summer.

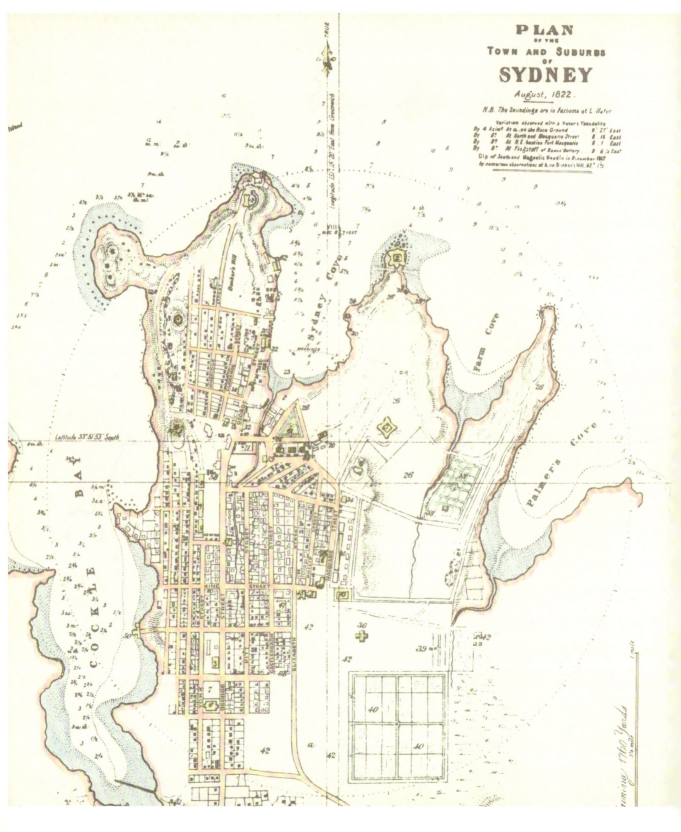

Despite Governor Phillip's best intentions, lack of Government funds from England prevented him from carrying out his ambitious plans for making Sydney a handsome city. It grew haphazardly, streets higgledy-piggledy, often narrow and clogged with dirt and mud. By 1810 Governor Lachlan Macquarie had changed all that, sweeping away the worst of the streets and lanes, and giving the main thoroughfares their present names – York Street, Pitt Street, George Street, and so on, marked on this map of 1822. The map shows the public buildings completed to the design of convict architect Francis Greenway – the 'rum hospital', the barracks, St James's Church (opposite each other across new Macquarie Street). An obelisk has been set up in Macquarie Place from which all distances from Sydney were to be measured, and a fine road sweeps out towards to Parramatta, with a toll-gate which was the cause of some dissention. Between Elizabeth Street and a large garden tended by the convicts, Hyde Park (so named by Macquarie) is designated as a race-course – and while Government House was actually still a dilapidated building in Bridge Street, the site of the present building is marked, while the Governor's stables (now the Conservatorium of Music) are already complete.

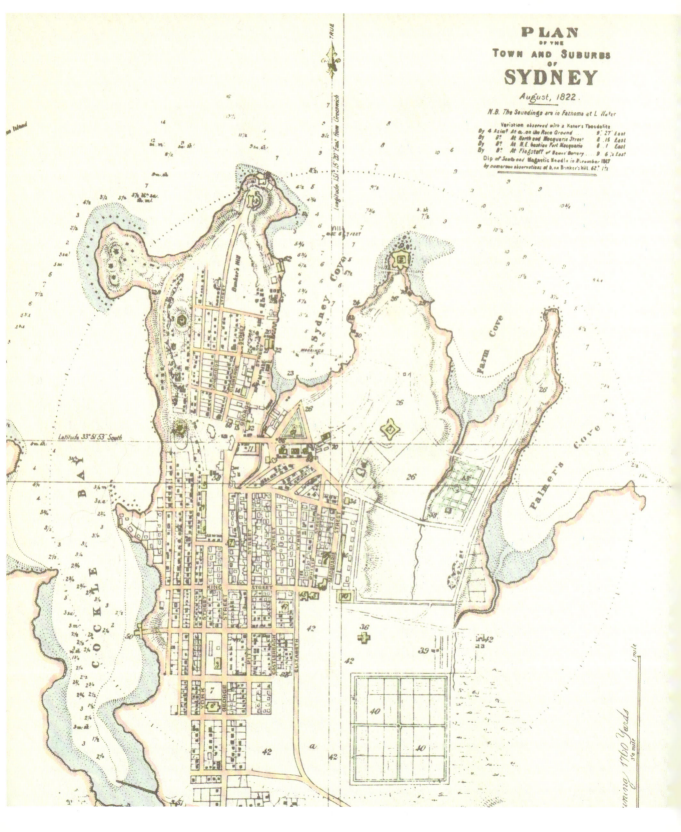

By 1854 the centre of Sydney, put in order by Governor Macquarie only forty years previously, had grown almost beyond recognition. The thorough and beautifully drawn map published that year by Woolcott and Clarke shows the growth of the city out beyond Ultimo and Darlinghurst, Chippendale and Surry Hills. Hyde Park, no longer a race-course, is properly laid out and St Mary's Cathedral has appeared to its east. St Andrew's is also marked, though no town hall is yet to be seen on the site of the burial ground next door. Nor has the QVB appeared on the site of the market a little further to the north. Semi-Circular Quay has an unfamiliar ring, but Cockle Bay has become Darling Harbour. Fort Macquarie occupies Bennelong Point, with Government House to the south (and a Governor's Bathing House conveniently nearby). The new Darlinghurst Gaol, still incomplete, seems almost in the country – as do the military barracks nearby. All this is meticulously drawn by the cartographers but their skill is unequal to portraying the confused hugger-mugger of the narrow streets and alleys of the Rocks, where 107 'disorderly houses' (i.e., brothels) were resorts for 'low strumpets', and the filth and lack of proper drains provided ideal conditions for the plagues which were waiting to break out.

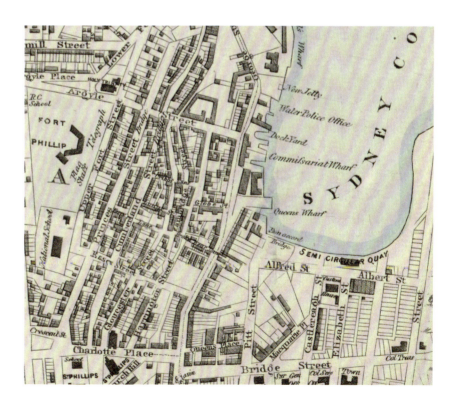

INDEX

A
Admiralty House 86
Ainslie 112
Albert, HRH Prince 116
Alice Street, Rosehill 8
Alfred Street 106
Ambassadors Café, the 146
Ambulance Avenue 158
Argyle Cut, the 66, 96
Argyle Street 96
Askin, Robert 214
ASTROGRAPHIC Calendar, the 105
Athol Gardens 176
Australia Square 2
Australian 54
Aust
zralian Steam Conveyance Co. 176
Australian Technology Park 134

B
Babworth House 166
Balmain East 176
Balmain New Ferry Co. 176
Balmain Road 138
Balmoral 190
Barangarooix
Barnet, James 42, 106, 112
Baronia House 156
bathing, nude 110
bathroom, an ingenious 54
Belmore Markets 188
Bennelong Point 90, 106, 212
Bent, Jeffrey Hart 34
Bent Street 200
Blacket, Edmund 66
Blair, Gorrie McLeish 200
Bligh, Governor William 12
Block, the, see Dymocks
Blues Point Tower 218
Bigge, J. T. 48, 50
Blacket, Edmund 100, 106
Blore, Edward 90
boar, Florentine 34
Bourke, Governor Sir Richard 90
Bond, Alan 208
Bond, Albert 116
Bondi 190
Boy Charlton Pool 110
Bradfield Highway 194
Bradfield, J. C. 194
Bradleys Head 128
Bradridge, Thomas and Edward 116
Brenan, John Ryan 138
Bridge Street 36
Brighton le Sands 190
Brisbane, Governor Thomas 16
Bristol 44
Brooks, Rachel and Thomas 132
Broughton House 138
Broughton, Bishop Norman 96
Brown, Hutchinson Hothersal 106

Buckeridge, J. H. 48
Buckingham Palace 90
Builders Labourers Federation, the 22
Burns Bay 132
Busserah Merchant, the 60

C
Cadman's Cottage 26, 106
Cadman, Elizabeth 26
Cadman, John 26
Cahill, Josph 212
Callan Park 138
Camden Park House 6
Campbell, Pieter Laurentz 74
Campbell Street 188
Cape Banks 128
Capitol Theatre 188
'Captain Moonlight' 84
Carisbrook House 132
Castlereagh Street 170
Cenotaph 172
Centennial Hall 116, 120
Centennial Park 2
Central Station 158
Challis House 170
Chalmers Street, Surry Hills 70
chandelier, 'Koh-i-Nor' 188
Charles, HRH Prince 92
Charlton, Andrew 'Boy' 110
Chequers nightclub, the 146
Chifley, Ben 208
Chifley Plaza 208
Chifley Square 208
Chifley Tower 208
Circular Quay 2, 36, 106, 142, 196
City rat-catcher 154
Cleveland Street School 66-68
clocks, tasteless 150
College Street, Darlinghurst 70
Collins, Capt. David 2
Colonial Mutual Life Assurance Society 170
Colonial Secretary's Building 106
Commonwealth Bank 170, 182
Condamine Street 220
Convicts' accommodation 46
Cooper, Robert 58
Cowper, Rev. W. 96
crime and prostitution 20
Crows Nest Farm 52
Cuddlepie 180
Cumberland Street 196
Cureton, Edward 36

D
Daily Telegraph building 182
Darling, Governor Ralph 60
Darlinghurst Gaol 80-84
Darling Point 166
Dawes Point 20, 96, 124, 194
Dawes, Second-Lieut. William 102
Dawson, Alexander 102, 106

Denison, Governor Sir William 102, 142
Destitute Children, Society for the Relief of 58
Devonshire Regiment 96
Devonshire Street 158
Diana, Princess of Wales 92
Dobell, William 188
Domain Baths 110
Dom, the 110
Don Bank 52
Dorman Long & Co. 194
Dublin 12
Dunavy, Price 188
Dusseldorp, Dick 218
Dymocks Building 182-84

E
Eberson, John 188
Eddy Avenue 158
Elizabeth Bay House 76
Elizabeth Farm 6
Elizabeth II, H.M. Queen 16, 92, 120, 214
Elizabeth Street 170, 188, 208
Essex Street 20
Eveleigh Railway Yards 134
executions, public 80
Experiment Farm Cottage 74

F
Fairfax, John 2
Fairyland 176
ferry wharves 176
Fig Tree, the 110
First Fleet, the 30, 36, 42, 102, 142, 212
Flagstaff Hill 102
Forbes Street, Darlinghurst 80
Fort Denison 102, 142-4
Fortifications, the 128-10
Fort Phillip 102
Fowler, Frank 20
Fraser, Alexander 74
Fraser's Disinfecting Apparatus 64
Freeman, Sir Ralph 194

G
Garrison Church 96-100
Garry Owen House 138
General Post Office see Sydney G.P.O.
George Street 20, 26, 106, 120, 146, 150; gaol, 80
Georges Head 128
Gibbs, May 180
Gibbes, J. G. N.
gin, benefits of 58
Gipps, Governor George 26, 90
Godwin, George William 156
Goosens, Sir Leon 212
Government Printer 46
Government House, Sydney 2, 12, 36, 90, 226
Government House, Parramatta 12
Green Bans 22, 76
Greenway, Francis 12, 26, 30, 42, 46, 48, 90, 194, 226
Greenwich 102

H

hauntings 60
Hale, Alfred H. 190
Hallen, Edward 66
Halloran, Laurence 66
Harbour Bridge see Sydney Harbour Bridge
Harnett, Richard Haynes 156
Harris, John 74
Harris Farm 74
Haslams Creek Cemetery 112
Hay Street 188
Hayes, Sir Henry Browne 54
Henry, Lucien 120
Heritage Act, the 52
Heritage Council 132, 156
Hill and Son 188
Hippodrome, the 188
Historic Houses Trust, the 2, 8, 34, 54
Holy Trinity Church, Sydney, see Garrison Church
Hordern, Sir Samuel 166
Hughes, Davis 214
Hunter, Governor John 12
Hunter Street 208
Hyde Park 44, 226
Hyde Park Barracks 44-6

I

Ifould, William Herbert 200
Isaacs, Governor-General Sir Isaac 86
Ipoh Garden 154

J

Jenkins, Capt. Benjamin 52
John Knox, the 52
Juniper Hall 58

K

Kearey, John and Michael 156
Keck, Henry 80
Kemp, W. E. 70
Kinchela, John 58
King, Governor Philip Gidley 12, 102, 128
King Street 50
Kirkbride, Dr Thomas 138
Kirkpatrick, John 34
Kirribilli Avenue, Kirribilli 86
Kirribilli House 86
Kirribilli Point 86
Kurraba Point 142

L

Lake, J. W. H. 180
Lane Cove Council 132
Lang, Jack 196
lavatory, art nouveau 36
Lawson, Henry 84
Legislative Council, the 30
Lewis, Mortimer William 80
Lightoller, Charles 143
Liverpool 44
Loftus Street 38
Loundon, J. C. 132
Lyons Patent Steam Disinfector 64

M

Macdonald, William 166
Macdonaldtown 134
Macfarlane's 38
Macleay Street 76
Macquarie, Elizabeth 12
Macquarie, Governor Lachlan ix, 12, 20, 26, 30, 36, 38, 42, 44, 48, 90, 200, 226
Macquarie Place 36, 226
Macquarie Street 34, 200, 208
Macquarie's Lighthouse 42, 44
Macarthur, John 6, 8
Macarthur, Elizabeth 6, 8
Mackennal, Sir Bernard 172
Majestic Theatre, Newtown 188
Manly Steamship Co. 176
Manning Street 76
Mansfield, G. A. 66
Mariners' Church see Garrison Church
Market Street 188
Martin Place 2, 170, 172, 182
Master in Lunacy, the 46
May-te-warm-ye see Fort Denison
McMahon's Point 218
McRae, George 153
Middle Head 128
Military Road 128, 156
Milsons Point 194, 196
Mint Museum, the, see Rum Hospital
Mitchell, David Scott 200
'moderated Romanesque' 70
Moore, Lieut. Thomas 206
Morgan, Francis 142
Morrow and De Ptron 156
Mort, Thomas Sutcliffe 38
Moore, Charles 138
Mortuary Temple, the 112
Mosman 156, 176
Mount Adelaide House 166
Mrs Macquarie's Road 110

N

Napier Street, N. Sydney 52
National Art School 80
National Trust, the 16, 58, 74, 188
Necropolis, the 112, 124
Nepean River 206
Newcastle 26
New South Wales Parliament House see Rum Hospital
New South Wales Writers' Centre 138
Nielsen, Juanita 76
Nightingale, Florence 34
North Fort 128
North Head 60, 128
North Head Scenic Drive, Manly 64
Northumberland Fusiliers 96
North Sydney 52
Nudity, public 110, 190
Nurses' Walk 30
Nutcote 180

O

Observatory, see Sydney Observatory
Observatory Hill 105
Oceana 120
O'Hearden, John 30
Old Government House see Government House, Parramatta
Old Pittwarer Road 220
Onslow Avenue 76
Opera House, The 211-14
orchestra, prisoners' 14
Ormond Hall see Juniper Hall
Oxford Street 58

P

Paddington 58
Palace of Democracy, the 116
parlatorio 60
Parramatta 74, 158
Parramatta River 176
Parramatta Park 16
Perpetual Trustee Co. Building 182
Petrarch 54
Philadelphia 80
Phillip, Governor Arthur 2, 12, 30, 36, 42, 74, 90, 142, 226
Phillip Street 106, 208
pig farm, convicts' 80
Pinchgutsee Fort Denison
Pitt Street 148, 172
plague, the 20
Port Jackson 26, 42, 52, 86, 110, 128
Port Jackson Steam Boat Co. 176
Potts Point 76-78
Powerhouse Museum 105, 158
Prince Albert Road 70
prostitution 80

Q

Qantas Buiolding 208
Quarantine Station 60-64
Queens Square 46
Queen Victoria Building 150-54

R

Redfern 134
Regent Street 112
Rocks, the 20, 30, 44, 96
Rocks Push, the 20
Rockwell House 76
Rookwood 112; and see Necropolis, the
Roselands Shopping Centre 220
Rowe, Thomas 34
Royal Irish Regiment 96
Royal West Kent Regiment 96
Rum Hospital, the 30, 44
Ruse, James 74
Ruse Street, Harris Park, Parramatta 74
Russell, Henry Chamberlain 102

S

St Andrew's Cathedral 116
St James's Church, Sydney 46, 48-50
St James's Theatre 188
St John's Church, Parramatta 12
St Leonard's 52
St Matthew's Church, Windsor 44
St Philip's Church, Sydney 96, 106
Sapsford, Thomas 110
Scott, Sir Walter 90
Scott, William 102
Seidler, Harry 172, 218 and see Blues Point Tower
Sheerin and Hennessy 156
Sirius, HMS 36, 42
smallpox 60
Smith, Rev. Isaac Carr 50
Snugglepot 180
South Head 128
Southwell, Daniel 42
Spencer, John 146
Spring Cove 60
stables, Government House 90, 226
Stanley Street 66

State Library   200-02
State Theatre   188
Steam Packet, the   26
Steel Point   128
Strand Arcade, the   146
Supreme Court building   46
Sydney College see Sydney Grammar School
Sydney College of the Arts   138
Sydney Conservatorium of Music   90, 226
Sydney Cove Redevelopment Authority   22
Sydney Dispensary   34
Sydney Ferries   176
Sydney Ferry Wharves see Ferry Wharves
Sydney General Post Office   2, 106, 170
Sydney Grammar School   66
Sydney Harbour Bridge   22, 52, 194-96
Sydney Harbour Federation Trust   128
Sydney Harbour National Park   26
Sydney Morning Herald   52, 190
Sydney Observatory   20, 60, 102-4, 108
Sydney Town Hall   116-20, 124
Sydney University   66
Sydney Water   2
Sydney Water Police   26
Swann, William and Elizabeth   8

T
Tait, Thomas   195
Tank Stream, the   2, 36
Tank Stream Fountain, the   2
Tanner, Howard   120
Taronga Zoo   176
Telopea   156
Tenhel, James   142
The Esplanade, Balmoral   190
Thomson, Robert   52
Time-ball, the   102
Titanic, the   143
Top Ryde   220
Trollope, Anthony   128
Turramurra artists' community   50
Tusculum   76

U
Ultimo   74
Utzon, J

V
Vaucluse House   54
Vaux, Calvert   132
Vernon, W.   158
'vice and immorality'   20
Victoria, H.M. Queen   2, 42, 90
Victoria Street, Potts Point   76

W
Wallaringa Avenue   180
Warragamba Dam   206-8
Warringah Mall   220
water closet, a distinguished   90
Waterhouse, B. J.   180
Water Police Court   106-8
Watson Road   105
Watson, Robert   42
Watsons Bay   176
Watts, Lieut. John   12
Weights and Measures Dept.   46
Wentworth, D'Arcy, 34
Wentworth Road, Vaucluse   54
Wentworth, William Charles   54
Westpac Bank   172
White, Frank Lloyd   190
White, Henry Eli   188
Wilson, F. H. B.   182
Wilson, J. H.   116
Wilson Street   134
Windsor   44
Windmill Hill   102
Woolloomooloo   80, 110
Woolloomooloo Hill see Potts Point
Wotongasee Admiralty House
Wunderlich Co.   184
Wurlitzers, mighty   188
Wynyard Station, 124

Y
York, HRH Duke of   146
York Street   150

Z
Zabul, Vincenz   156

PHOTOGRAPHY IN THIS BOOK

The majority of the photographs were taken by and are copyright © the authors, Derek and Julia Parker.

The authors and publishers would like to thank the following people and organisations who additionally supplied photography and map images for the indicated pages.

Cover (left hand photograph): Sally Mayman, courtesy Tourism NSW; i (frontispiece), 19, 21, 25, 106, 212, 215: Simon Dance; 1: Daniel Boud; 3, 17, 101, 225/226, 227/228: Mitchell Library; 5: 3 Stroke Photography, courtesy Tourism NSW; 7d, 22b: Veechi Stuart; 9, 113, 193, 200: State Library of NSW; 11, 13, 15, 39, 73, 74, 95, 97, 103, 133, 135, 137, 161: Robbie Begg; 23, 45b, 47, 96, 134: Derek & Julia Parker; 27: John Merriman; 43: Grenville Turner, courtesy Tourism NSW; 83: Peter Liebeskind; 99, 143, 146, 153, 211: Hamilton Lund, courtesy Tourism NSW; 105, 150: Tourism NSW; 145: Isabel Rosero; 147: Tony Yeates, courtesy Tourism NSW; 151: City of Sydney Archive; 170-171: Commonwealth Bank; 181: Albert Nghiem; 187: Ross Thorne; 194: Darroch Donald; 199: Wildlight, courtesy Tourism NSW; 214: Gerry Colley (Turtle Pictures), courtesy Tourism NSW; 221: Dee Why Public Library; 223: National Library of Australia.

Except where out of copyright, all photographs are copyright © the photographers or suppliers and may not be reproduced without permission.

OTHER TITLES FROM WOODSLANE PRESS

Building Sydney's History is just one of a growing series of books from Australian publishers Woodslane Press.
To browse through other titles available from Woodslane Press, including the Boiling Billy imprint, visit www.woodslaneonline.com.au.
If your local bookshop does not have stock of a Woodslane Press book, they can easily order it for you. In case of difficulty please contact our customer service team on 02 9970 5111 or info@woodslane.com.au. Titles include:

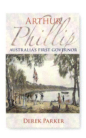

Arthur Phillip

$44.95 (hardback)

ISBN: 9781921203992

Building Brisbane's History

$34.95

ISBN: 9781921606199

Bligh in Australia

$24.95

ISBN: 9781921683503

Sydney's Best Harbour & Coastal Walks

$29.95

ISBN: 9781921606274

Governor Macquarie

$24.95

ISBN: 9781921606915

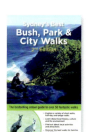

Sydney's Best Bush, Park & City Walks

$29.95

ISBN: 9781921683626